Trust and Wonder

A Waldorf Approach to Caring for Infants and Toddlers

Eldbjørg Gjessing Paulsen

WALDORF EARLY CHILDHOOD ASSOCIATION OF NORTH AMERICA

First English Edition
© 2011 Waldorf Early Childhood Association of North America
Trust and Wonder: A Waldorf Approach to Caring for Infants and Toddlers
ISBN: 978-1-936849-03-1

This publication was made possible by a grant
from the Waldorf Curriculum Fund.

Illustration: Carsten Andersen
Photo Editor: Eldbjørg Gjessing Paulsen
Translator: Ingrid Andersen
Editors: Eldbjørg Gjessing Paulsen, Ann Sharfman
English Edition Editor and Graphic Design: Lory Widmer

Thanks!

There have been many people who have followed and given me inspiration in the process of creating this book: children, colleagues, friends and family.

Thank you to all of you.

Thanks to Brit Østerud and Tone Bergan who supported me along the road.

Thanks to Reidun Iversen who gave me the courage to finish the book.

Thanks to my sister Ingrid who said yes to do the translating of the book.

Thanks to Ann Sharfman for helping me in editing the English version.

Thanks to Lory Widmer for her work on the English edition and to the Waldorf Curriculum Fund for financial support.

This book is dedicated to my children and grandchildren

Contents

7	**Foreword**
9	**Introduction: "To meet a child's gaze"**
15	**Chapter 1: The Fourfold Human Being**
21	**Chapter 2: Child Development in the First Three Years**

The child's first year: The first steps towards independence 25
The child's second year: The first words are formed 28
The child's third year: The first thoughts awaken 31

35	**Chapter 3: The Adult's Responsibility Toward the Child Today**

Creating a peaceful and protected environment 38
Recognizing the power of imitation 39
Being a role model 41
Providing opportunities to explore and practice new skills 43

45	**Chapter 4: The Child as a Sense Being**

The sense of touch 49
The sense of life 51
The sense of self-movement 51
The sense of balance 53
Conclusion 55

57	**Chapter 5: Rhythm and Time in the Child's Daily Routine**

The significance of rhythm in the child's development 60
Taking time for children 62
Creating a good daily routine 65
A day in the kindergarten 67
Weekly and yearly rhythms in the kindergarten 72

Contents

75   **Chapter 6: The Child's Play**
Toys and equipment for play   79

81   **Chapter 7: The Physical Environment**
The indoor environment   84
Form and color   84
The coatroom   86
The main room/kitchen   87
The changing room   88
The sleeping room   88
The outdoor environment   89

93   **Chapter 8: Models for Infant and Toddler Groups**
Sibling group   95
Toddler group within the kindergarten   96
Infant and toddler group   98

99   **Chapter 9: Working with Parents and Other Caregivers**
Teamwork between home and kindergarten   101
Everyday conversations   102
Parent/teacher meetings   103

107   **Chapter 10: Working with Colleagues**
Daily teamwork   110
Staff meetings   111

113   **Conclusion**

117   **Bibliography**

121   **Appendix: Two Lullabies from South Africa**

123   **About the Author**

Foreword

Early childhood experiences leave footprints, both good and bad, in all people's lives. Whatever happens to us on the road from birth until we can stand on our own two feet will make a strong imprint on our biography. The first three years are of more importance than any other period in a human being's life. During these years, the child has the potential to develop his abilities and gifts, provided that he is in an environment that is safe, and where he feels physically and psychologically well and socially supported.

To do this the child needs adults with the ability to observe when he has a need for protection, for comfort, and for encouragement. It is this kind of fundamental safety that gives the child the possibility to grow and develop in freedom.

Through my work with children as a mother and a Waldorf teacher, I have had many experiences that have shown me the importance of the first three years. I have thought long and hard as to whether it is the right thing to welcome the child under three into the kindergarten, and it has taken me a long, long time to be able to say "Yes" to this question. My experience and knowledge of Waldorf education over more than twenty years have been the most important driving force in shaping the thoughts and methods that I want to pass on in this book.

Today Waldorf nursery/kindergartens are found all over the world, both in developed countries and in countries where poverty and needs are prominent. In spite of different cultures and circumstances these kindergartens have a common base in Rudolf Steiner's philosophy, understanding of the human being, and pedagogical impulse, which form a foundation for the educational methods.

Most of the Waldorf nursery/kindergartens around the world started with children from three to seven years of age, for four to five hours each day. In the meantime there have been major changes in Norway and other countries, both in the ages of the children and the operating hours of the kindergarten. Some countries have had groups for toddlers for many years, but in Norway only recently have the needs of the toddler group been recognized. Out of the needs of the parents and of society, more and more Waldorf kindergartens have begun caring for toddlers.

In Stjerneglimt Waldorf Kindergarten in Norway, where I have worked since its inception in 1984, we started caring for babies and toddlers in the year 2000. One of the main reasons for writing this book has been the wish to share some of the experiences we have had on this journey. In addition, I would like to share with you our discoveries regarding caring for the very young group as opposed to the older children in our kindergartens and homes.

We started with a small group of infants and toddlers who were integrated into a group of older children. After a year we started a group for children under three. This group has become the "heart" of the kindergarten. It radiates warmth and the very special atmosphere surrounding the smallest children, which we endeavor to preserve throughout the kindergarten years.

My respect for the child and for our responsibility as educators has grown over the years. The purpose of this book is not to give answers to all possible questions, but to awaken an interest in how we can see and understand what babies and toddlers need.

The book is meant as an inspiration to parents, educators, teachers, and caregivers who wish to have a deeper understanding of the child under the age of three and for those who wish to start their own infant/toddler group. ♡

Note to the English Edition
Many different names are possible for Waldorf early childhood settings that include the youngest children. For the sake of simplicity, we have followed the author's experience in referring to a younger group or section within a larger kindergarten.

Introduction

"To meet a child's gaze"

"To meet a child's gaze"

The child

To meet a child's gaze
Is more than a meeting of springtime
It's like going on a journey
Back tens of thousands of years
Not only to find your own childhood again
But to search for childhood
In the dawn of time[1]
—Andre Bjerke, Norwegian Poet
   Translated by Eldbjørg Gjessing Paulsen

I have chosen this poem by Andre Bjerke as an introduction to our journey into the child's world in the first three years. The poem encapsulates the essential core, the heart of childhood, which is so important for teachers, parents, and other adults in meeting the little child. It is with wonder and awe that we face the child who comes into this world with the greatest faith and overwhelming trust. At that same time that we experience something new and unfinished in a baby, we may also experience an ancient wisdom.

During the first three years of life, the foundation is laid for becoming a human being. The baby comes to us with absolute trust that we will take care of her life and her growth, and that what we provide will always be right. We need to have the same trust and wonder in order to meet the child, and to observe and support her development.

---

1 Andre Bjerke, *Fakkeltog*, p. 26.

The meeting of eyes has a meaning for all of us—it reveals the ego or identity of another. We can sense unknown possibilities or forces, or obstacles or resignation; we sense when someone has given up or is discouraged. It is easier to meet some people than others through eye contact. A lot can happen through eye contact; it is like being touched, especially when there is a special way of looking and meeting with the eyes.

When a parent looks in a baby's eyes it forms the foundation of the first meeting between baby and mother or father. Often even from the outside one can feel the mantle of love that encompasses this meeting.

In his book *Barnet's Verden* (The Child's World) Arve Mathiesen, a Norwegian Waldorf teacher, writes: "It is noteworthy that the children look us in the eye as soon they can control their eye movements. How do they know that the adults see the eyes as the 'mirror of the soul'? What is it that makes the child seek out this contact? One would assume that eye contact is the result of maturing and not the starting point for the newborn. Or is this the way the child's individuality seeks contact with the adult's individuality?"[2] To meet the child through the eye makes me ask the questions:

Who are you?
Where do you come from?
And where are you going in your life?
What are the tasks that you have come to fulfil while you are on the earth?
And what are the tasks I must fulfil in my time with you as a guide?
Can I be part of your journey? What is it that brings the two of us together?
How can I contribute in a way that helps you, in your own way, to develop your possibilities?
How can I help you to overcome the challenges and obstacles that you will meet?
What is it that I am going to learn from you so that I too will develop myself as a human being?
What about my own childhood?

There are many more questions that we can ask ourselves when we meet the youngest human beings. To find some of the answers, we need concrete knowledge of human development—both physical and psychological. There is much knowledge and many books that give information about human development and good advice as to how we should educate our own and other people's children. Our own memories from

---

2 Arve Mathiesen, *Barnet's Verden*, p. 28.

childhood can contribute towards confirming or disproving the many theories surrounding this theme. Nevertheless, it is the children themselves who can best give us the answers as to what they need for their development.

By observing a child's being and attitude we can find some of the answers. It could also be important to remember how we ourselves reacted to various sensory experiences. The essence of the human being's knowledge of human nature comes from knowing one's self and one's own development. For me, the knowledge and understanding of a spiritual world is a great help in finding an overall picture both of the child and our task as educators. The thought that the whole human being, not just the physical aspect, develops both before and after birth makes a wider understanding of the development of the child possible.

One "picture" for this thought can be the birthday story that is told in many Waldorf kindergartens. There are many ways of telling this story depending on which child the story is meant for and who the storyteller is. The story tells about a little child who is in heaven together with his or her guardian angel before birth, and is waiting to come down to earth. This waiting time is used by the child for something that is essential to the human being—for *play*.

One way of telling a birthday story:

The child is playing with a ball, throwing it up into the air and catching it. This happens again and again until one day the ball is gone. The child searches everywhere for the ball and discovers a small hole in a fence. Being curious, as all children are, the child has to look through the hole and there is able to look all the way down to the earth. Then a place or house appears that looks so inviting—warm and cosy—and the child wants to go down at once to live there. But the time has not come yet. Time goes by and the child is asking the guardian angel to please to let him or her go down to the earth. But the answer always is to wait until everything is ready.

Down on the earth a mummy and a daddy are waiting for the child and preparing everything. They are so excited and full of joy that the child will soon be with them, and finally the time arrives. The guardian angel follows the child to the heavenly gateway, and from there the child has to go on his or her own, traveling on a rainbow and passing all the stars, the sun, and the moon until the earth is very near. The child falls into a deep sleep and the mother knows that the time has come for her baby to be born. At first the baby knocks softly, then more strongly, and finally very strongly and then the child is born.

The mummy and the daddy look in wonder and see that a little girl (or boy) has come to them. When they look closer they see that it is "Anna" (or "John"—the child's name). The joy is so great that they have to share it with everybody who has been waiting for this *little child.*

Even though this story is not told to children under three years old, and so does not belong outwardly to the framework of this book, it is a picture that we adults can carry with us. The picture shows the children's connection with the spiritual world, from whence they come, and which in many ways is still their home. It also tells us how welcome the children are and that someone has waited just for each "Anna" or "John." No matter what kind of family the child is coming to, it is important for every child to become aware of the fact that someone has waited for him and was glad that he was born. For us as adults and educators it is important that we receive the child with respect and reverence. The intimacy and closeness that happens when we meet the child "in the eyes" then builds a bridge for the child into the earthly world through human interaction. ♥

Chapter One

The Fourfold Human Being

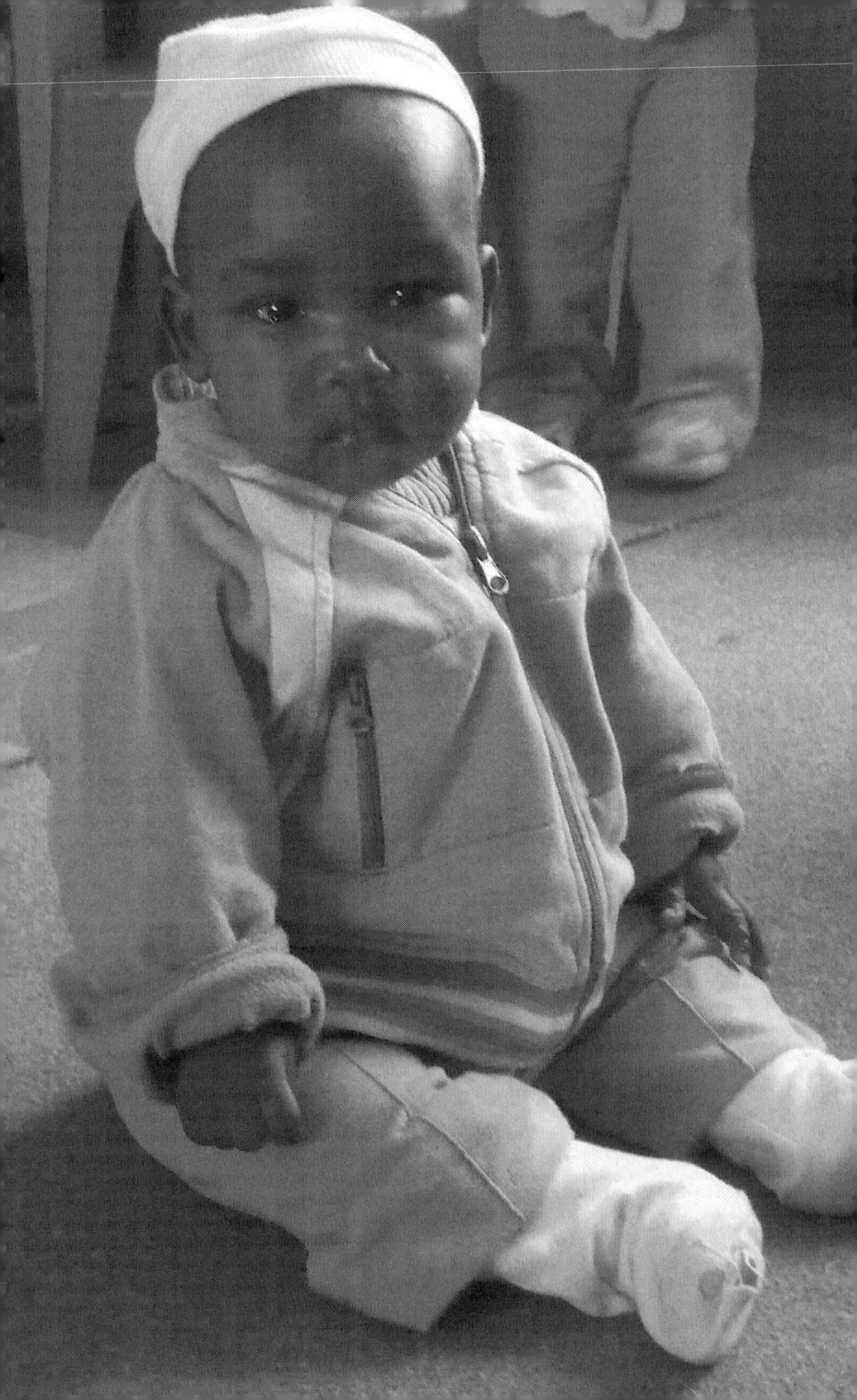

The Fourfold Human Being

The philosophy of Rudolf Steiner is known as Anthroposophy (from *Antropos* = the human being, *Sophia* = wisdom). Anthroposophical knowledge of humankind is a valuable tool for enabling adults to assist the child in building a connection with the world. The child's successful development into a free-thinking and independent human being is totally dependent on connecting with and knowing other people and the world.

The following is a short synopsis of Rudolf Steiner's view of the four "bodies" of the human being, which is important to understanding the anthroposophical view of child development and Waldorf education. An understanding of this and other aspects of Anthroposophy can be broadened and deepened by consulting further literature on the topic. A short list of suggested reading is included at the end of this book.

Anthroposophy states that during earthly life the human being has four sheaths: the physical body, the etheric (life) body, the sentient (astral) body and the I-body/ego.

The first element is **the physical body**, which is based on the inherent laws of the mineral world.

The second element is the **etheric** or **life body**, shared in common with the plant and animal kingdoms. Everything that lives has a life body, which supports growth, healing, and reproduction. Compare a plant and a stone, and the "force of life" is immediately apparent.

The third element is the **astral** or **sentient body**, which we have in common with the animals. Here we find desires, reluctance, pain, pleasure, love, dislikes, instincts, and other aspects of the soul. Through this body the sense-perceptible world is taken in and becomes inner experience, and we can also sense the feelings of other people and animals.

The fourth and highest element is the **ego** or **I**, which is unique to the human being. It bears the spiritual kernel of the human being, which has the opportunity to grow and develop through incarnating in a physical body (that is also endowed with life and soul). The I, as my own individuality or awareness of my "self," is experienced or known through the meeting with another's I.

Rudolf Steiner says in his book *The Education of the Child*:

> *No one can use this name to designate another. Every human being can only call themselves 'I'; the name 'I' can never reach my ear as a description of myself. In designating oneself as I, one has to name oneself within oneself. Human beings who can say 'I' are a world unto themselves. Those religions founded on spiritual knowledge have always had a feeling for this truth; hence they have said, 'With the I, the God, who in lower creatures reveals himself only externally in the phenomena of the surrounding world, begins to speak internally.'*[3]

When we understand the nature of the ego, we see that the child is not an unwritten page when she arrives in the world. She comes with hidden knowledge and wisdom from the spiritual world. We cannot actually "teach" the child anything in the first few years. We can only arrange a healthy environment and behave in the right way in front of her. These are the years of self-development, when the child moves from phase to phase through her own efforts, and while doing so acquires knowledge through the opportunities we provide. Children don't only imitate what we say and do, but who we are as people, good and bad. The child has an ability to see through us and see who we are as human beings.

We cannot, and should not, attempt to change the individuality of the child. What we can do is to provide the right conditions for her to explore her own capabilities and the world around her. To "assist" children means to guide them to utilize their inborn abilities and to overcome obstacles.

Development does not only belong to the early years. We keep on developing throughout life and constantly have the opportunity to change ourselves and the world around us. The sense of self affects actions, feelings and thoughts. The ego carries the whole human being, body and soul. It plays out in different phases throughout life, and we all need to go through these phases. According to Rudolf Steiner, the ego is not fully developed until the age of twenty-one. Waldorf teach-

---

[3] Rudolf Steiner, *The Education of the Child*, p. 10.

ing emphasizes that we should always bear in mind that human beings are different at various stages in life and need to be met accordingly.

A vital realization in this regard is that birth is not a singular event. Our physical body is born at the moment of what we call birth, but the three other sheaths are still undergoing a further development before they reach a certain level of independence and freedom. These "births" occur at approximately seven-year intervals, dividing childhood into three seven-year periods.

During the first period, from birth to seven, the life body is still strongly bound to the physical body. It is responsible for the amazingly rapid growth and development that we see during this time. Around the age of seven part of the life forces are "born" and become available for other tasks, such as school learning. In Waldorf early childhood education it is considered of paramount importance to support the life body in its work, and to provide experiences that strengthen rather than deplete the life forces.

Our tools to accomplish this are:

Caring and love
Imitation
Role modeling
Good rhythm and habits
Healthy sense experiences and nurture of the senses
Right nutrition
Free movement possibilities
Rich language
Singing
Enough room for self-activity without too much interference or interruption from adults

The most important gift we can give in the early years is to allow the child to be *left in peace* to take his own steps into the world—one step at a time, at his own pace and in safety and security. This will give the child a good start in life and a solid basis for becoming an independent, creative, and thinking human being. ♡

# Chapter Two

Child Development in the First Three Years

There are three fundamental abilities that children have to acquire in the first three years of life that will affect their lives as adults. The child needs to stand independently—to become upright—and then to learn to walk; then, later, to begin to talk. The development of language is the foundation of the third ability, the ability to think.

How the learning process proceeds can vary from child to child, but all healthy children will learn to walk, talk, and think. Development follows a universal pattern and is independent of culture. However, even if the development of walking, talking, and thinking has a common pattern, the development of every child is totally dependent on the human beings that surround him, as well as on the environment provided.

What does a newborn baby need to feel welcomed and comfortable in the world? He needs the same kind of protection that he had in the mother's womb—he needs parents and caregivers who provide the vital primary requirements like loving care, warmth, physical contact, and healthy nutrition.

The parents or the primary caregivers have the most profound influence and responsibility in the baby's life. They have to ensure that the primary needs of their baby are met. They are there to help the child to incarnate into the physical world and to see that the conditions are favorable for a healthy and happy childhood.

Rudolf Steiner said, "Just as nature causes the proper environment for the physical body before birth, so after birth the educator must provide for the proper physical environment."[4]

---

4 Rudolf Steiner, *The Education of the Child*, p. 18.

One very important thing to realize in creating this environment is that the newborn baby comes to the earth as one big sense organ and needs to be protected against too many sense impressions. Everything that the child experiences has an effect on the physical body—for example, things that cause shock, like very loud sounds, strong light, or other sense impressions that are disturbing to the child.

Another vital realization is that human contact is just as important as food for the survival of an infant. Gentle touch that forms a relationship with another person is a form of nourishment to the child. Eye contact is an important part of relationship formation and makes the child feel that she belongs to somebody. When adults look into the eyes of a baby, they become aware that the baby gives herself without any holding back, in full trust to that person. We also experience this trust when we receive the first longed-for smile from a baby. Eyes meet, the smile follows, and love streams between the baby and the adult. The child's joy in being seen and acknowledged is reflected in her smile. This is very important for children's self-image or self-concept—not only in the first years, but for the rest of their lives. As adults, we also need this human recognition and acknowledgement from others. Through acknowledgement we feel valued and recognized as a person.

A newborn child is impossible not to take notice of, and can't be ignored. It's a miracle we experience every time we meet an infant. We feel respect, humility, and the need to protect the little wonder that's lying there ready for the world. We become quieter, the mood lightens, and our voice pitch heightens. We become softer. We can ask and wonder why we have this attitude towards a newborn. Is it about the unknown that we can barely sense? Or all the questions that arise: Where does this little being come from? What does she carry to give to the world? And what is the future that awaits *this* child?

So many questions arise, making us feel humble as we come near to a child. Our humility and interest, together with stillness, wonder, and respect, will hopefully last throughout the child's developing years. The baby must be taken care of by adults who have a deep respect and interest in observing where the child is on the developmental path.

The adult needs to know that the way the child is at any particular stage in these early times won't necessarily stay that way—in behavior, features, and so on. Development is an ongoing process, so when a two-year-old reaches the stage of defiance, it is helpful to recognise it as a stage that has to be gone through as a necessary part of growth toward independence and freedom. Parents and caregivers should welcome this stage, knowing that their child is moving forward and that this stage, like all others, will pass. This stage of life is mostly needed for the strength of the child's will. And, difficult though it may be, at this stage, as at any other, little ones need to be seen, acknowledged, and loved. Throughout our lives, this is what gives us a sense of safety and confidence in who we are and what we can achieve.

The child's first year: The first steps towards independence

Physical development during the first years is very noticeable. We see how the child grows and changes all the time. The infant *appears* perfect at birth. The body has head, chest, stomach, arms, legs—all the body parts are there. However, we need to know that the body is not fully developed. It has to grow, and the inner organs which are not fully formed at birth must develop and mature. During the first year, the child's weight doubles, and at the same time he is learning to stand upright and take his first steps. Both are great achievements, a miracle in such a short time.

During this period, the child needs all his energy and vitality to develop and structure the exterior body and the inner organs. The outer physical changes are visible during the early years; what is happening inside may not be visible, but is just as important. The innermost organs and the brain take shape and develop in the first years.

Rudolf Steiner says about the organs:

In this period the physical organs must form themselves into definite shapes; their whole structural nature must receive particular tendencies and directions. Growth takes place in later periods as well; but throughout the whole succeeding life growth is based on the forces developed in this first life period. If true forms were developed, true forces would grow; if misshapen forms were developed, misshapen forms would grow. We can never repair what we have neglected as educators in the first seven years; just as nature causes the proper environment for the physical human body before birth, so after birth the educator must provide for the physical environment. The right physical environment alone works on the child in such a way that the physical organs correctly shape themselves.[5]

Here "educator" can be taken to mean parents, caregivers, teachers—all adults in the child's environment.

---

[5] Rudolf Steiner, *The Education of the Child*, p. 18.

Physical growth is enormous during pregnancy. In the embryonic stage the head dominates and makes up more than half of the fetus at two months. In a newborn and for the first one and a half years, the head still forms about a quarter of the total body length. (In an adult, it is only one eighth).[6]

So in the small child the head still typically appears very large, arms and legs are shorter, and the form is round and soft. Within one to two years after birth a change takes place and the chest and stomach become prominent and plump. Now the body has grown more than the head. Up until three years of age, most children keep the round, soft forms of their bodies. This is very noticeable in the "dimples" on the back of the hand. As children grow older, these soft forms change and become more defined. The muscles become more visible.

Motor development happens individually, even though all children have to go through each one of the general phases. The mastery of the body slowly emerges. It starts with keeping the head up, discovering the hands and legs and how to use them, learning to sit, crawl and finally getting up on two legs to stand. In the beginning the movements seem to be involuntary and chaotic. Arms and legs move all over the place seemingly without any direction. After a while movements become more controlled, and begin to have a purpose. When the gaze has steadied, the infant discovers her hands and fingers and soon the feet also become interesting. The child is so flexible and soft that to put her toes in her mouth is a simple matter (something quite incredible from an adult's point of view).

Now the child sees something and wants to grab and touch it, and through constant repetition of these actions her coordination becomes stronger and stronger. On all fronts the child starts taking control of her own body and will eventually manage to sit and stand up. When exactly that happens is up to each individual, but as a general rule it takes place during the first year.

At birth, the child has no self-consciousness, but is still "sleeping." The child simply exists in his environment, unaware of the boundaries between self and world. After a while the child becomes aware of objects and will get to know his surroundings and his own place in them. This happens instinctively, but in time the child will coordinate grab-

---

6 Bernard Lievegoed, *Phases of Childhood*, p. 28.

bing with the sight of an object and it slowly becomes a conscious act. The child sees the ball and grabs it. The boundaries between the child and the world become more distinct.

The child uses enormous strength and life forces to master these physical abilities, with a perseverance and eagerness that we can only admire. He wants to conquer the world and does not give up! Even without an adult's influence, a child will try and try again in order to learn. Individuality determines *how* he masters one or another skill. Some learn quickly, others take longer, but there is a wide range of what is considered "normal."

At around six to eight months old, the child can sit, and then starts crawling from place to place. Suddenly the world has become *so* much bigger and there are even more things to touch and explore. One day the child discovers that she can hold on to something and pull herself up. Tables, chairs, Mum's dress, and Dad's trousers are all used to hoist herself up. Standing may only last for a second, before the child sits down again. This will happen every day until at last the big moment arrives when the child takes her first step out into the world and discovers "Here I am!" This is considered a milestone, not only for the child, but also for the proud adults who have followed the process with excitement. Usually this happens around one year of age, but can just as easily happen at eight or seventeen months.

The most important aspect is that the child has managed on her own, without any supporting help. Putting a child into a walking ring, for example, interferes with this important development. The deciding factor is not only the child's determination to get up, but the possibility of imitating human beings who are walking upright. When the child reaches the point where she can stand up on her own two feet and take her own first steps, she has the option to choose her own distance from or closeness to others. Meetings between people become very different when we have the freedom to choose how close we want to be. At this moment the child's first "step" toward freedom and independence has been taken.

In the Waldorf kindergarten we put great importance on the fact that babies will explore the world around them, and that, with role models and a safe environment, they will learn to walk. The most important factor is that *the child* decides when the time is right to take the first step and should be left alone to do so. Respectfully, we let children battle a bit and allow them to discover the joy of succeeding without being pushed. Our purpose, as adults, is to create a safe physical environment that gives enough time to master universal movements, to explore the world, and to develop skills. Much depends on the adult's attitude. We have to set a good example in deeds and words. How *we* move and behave is important for the child's process of learning to walk.

The child's second year: The first words are formed

Usually the first words are formed once the child starts walking. Up until then, the child has been using mainly gibberish sounds and signs.

Both children and adults have a body language, which is the first communication we have with other human beings. This remains a great influence on communication throughout life. Some children develop a body language that tells us what they want or what they want us to do for them. This can be positive; however, it might delay the act of talking. It is very important that adults use words even when they understand what the child wants. This will help the child to use words and start talking and not only using body language.

Through body language the child will report back about his being well or not. When an infant is hungry, it is often expressed through crying; when he is happy, he smiles and gurgles. The infant experiences likes and dislikes as a direct result of the environment. It can be people, animals, objects, or situations that the child experiences and reacts to. Later come feelings of happiness, anger, and sadness that are expressed in the spoken word in addition to body language. A one-year-old can feel joy and pain, but still cannot express them in words. We can interpret and understand what the child is trying to "say" through his behaviour and body language. This way we can meet the child's needs and understand what is required.

When language starts to develop, another world opens, full of possibilities for communication with others. In the same way that the child learned to walk, so he will learn to talk through imitation. Language opens enormous possibilities. We can name objects, put words to feelings and thoughts, share ideas and, importantly, we use them to connect with and understand others. Language is not something we inherit—we were not born with a language—but all children are born with the *ability* to learn a language. Even though the ability is there, that in it self is not enough. The child must be surrounded by people who are using a language that the child can imitate. In other words, adults' use of language is absolutely necessary for the development of the child's speech.

The dermatologist Ole Fyrand writes in his book *Berøring* (Touch):

> The German-Roman emperor Frederick (1194–1250) wanted to find out what was the original language of Man, so he demanded that some newborn babies should grow up without any human contact. Nobody was to speak to them in their own language. All the children died after a short while.[7]

This shows us not only how important language is, but also how incredibly necessary human contact is for the child to survive.

Several authors have touched on the importance of language for humans. The South African Nobel Prize winner for literature, Nadine Gordimer, said:

> Conservative, liberal and left-wing thinkers in contemporary schools of linguistic philosophy agree about one thing; man became man not by the tool but by the Word. It is not walking upright and using a stick to dig for food or strike a blow that makes a human being, it is speech. And neither intelligent apes nor dolphins whispering in the ocean share with us the ability to transform this direct communication and commune between peoples and generations who will never meet.[8]

Man's very identity, physical, psychological, and spiritual, is expressed through language.

During the first year, the larynx is developed so that it can be used as a language tool. At eight to ten weeks, the child starts making gurgling and babbling noises, especially when happy. These sounds are the same all over the world, regardless of which language the child is surrounded by. After a while, the child starts copying the language she hears. It becomes very important that adults use clear and correct language and don't succumb to the temptation to use "baby" talk. That does not mean that we must avoid the nonsense words that emerge; on the contrary, they are also valuable, but in another context.

The way that *we* use language, and connect it to movement, is a very important foundation for the language-learning process for the child. In the same way that the child learns to use her muscles to achieve standing and walking, so the muscles of the larynx must be trained to form words. The muscles around the larynx are drawn together and perform movements that correspond to those we do with our hands, fingers, legs, and body, thus becoming flexible. This is why

---

7 Ole Fyrand, *Berøring*, p. 54.
8 Quoted in Barry Sanders, *A Is for Ox*, p. 3.

it is so important that we connect words with movement, through verses, rhymes, and songs accompanied by movements that involve all parts of the child's body.

Individuality emerges when we observe how different children acquire language. Some are very excited and try to get an adult's attention by making sounds while pointing at something they want. Others try to repeat what they hear, but make their own noises and their own "language." In our kindergarten we had a little boy aged fourteen months. Every time his parents came to fetch him, he embarked on a long story that nobody understood. It sounded like he was telling his parents about everything that had happened in the kindergarten that day. We all listened and wondered.

The most important thing at this early stage is for the young child to "taste" the words, hear the sounds, and repeat what is said without necessarily understanding the meaning. The full meaning of words will become clearer later on in life. The main thing for an adult to do is to say the word attached to an object or person while indicating what the word refers to. We should also be aware that children not only hear the words that we say, they also sense the mood behind the words—whether happiness, sorrow or anger.

Around the age of eighteen months the child learns single-syllable words. Now everything in the surroundings will be named: mummy, daddy, cat, cup, chair. Words are used to get to know the world, to "own" it by naming it. The child begins to know the objects in the world in relation to herself. For example, here is "Maria," there is a chair, and so on.

In toddler groups in the Waldorf kindergarten, adults and children often enjoy song and play together. For instance, an adult will sit down on the carpet and start singing a song with accompanying movements. This is repeated every day at the same time, and it won't be long before the children sit down by themselves at same time every day and want to sing. This happens purely as a matter of choice. If some babies want to crawl away, they can. They can come and go as they please because they will join the singing when they are ready for it. The songs and rhymes are repeated week after week, sometimes throughout the whole year. "Baa, Baa Black Sheep" can be sung several times during the day, and the children never tire of it, even if the adults do! We can see the joy they experience and understand that this has a deeper meaning. The repetition of sound and rhythm is the secret, and the experience of recognizing the song has great appeal, especially to the youngest. You can see the enthusiasm each time. Enjoying the small things in life is important, as a foundation for new challenges.

The use of fairy tales is another way of imparting a rich and varying language. But we prefer to save the "real" storytelling until the children are three years old and then tell only the simplest tales. Children younger than three years have difficulty in following and concentrating when the action is too long and the concept too complicated. Their ability to imagine and "see" the story is only at the initial phase. That is why little ones love hearing stories that are short and simple and which relate to things we adults have experienced, either alone, or together with them. Stories about the little cat we saw on the way to kindergarten, or about the bird that sat on the bird feeder and ate crumbs, are the sort of stories they want to hear over and over again. They never get tired of repetition!

As language develops, conversations with children will have more content and their understanding of, and connection with, their surroundings will widen. It is very important that we have patience when speaking with children, for many need a long time to find the right words to express the experience they have had. Often a word or a simple sentence will help them convey what's in their heart. When we connect words to action, it aids understanding and builds language. We can say: "Come, let's find your shoes and put them on," or "Here are your socks." All the time our presence and attention directed towards the child will help the development of language and healthy growth in general.

The child's third year: The first thoughts awaken

During the third year of life, the child starts to understand language more and more. At the same time the child realizes that he is being understood when he communicates. Now it's not only about body language. Vocabulary has increased and sentences are becoming longer. Memory is strengthened through constant repetition and the routine habits of every day. The child's thoughts and actions are connected to experiences through recognition and repetition. Only when the word and object, or word and concept, are connected, is an inner picture able to be formed.

The child discovers himself as part of, but separate from, his surroundings during the first years. As the child's understanding of the separate identity of himself as opposed to objects around him becomes more distinct, an awakening takes place. The first thought processes come into being as the child, through his interactions, begins to make his own pictures of the outer world.

The child has sense impressions of his own. Impressions will first be connected to the "I-consciousness" that makes a child react individually and not only through reflex or instinct. It's the beginning of "myself and my own world view." Throughout, these pictures metamorphose and can appear as conscious thoughts at later stage. The development is from picture-formation to conceptualization, then on to pure thought processes. Experiencing and partaking in various real-life work processes that can easily be seen and, therefore, understood, helps to create a solid foundation on which to build thought processes.

Through logical actions we lay the foundation for logical thinking. By repeating sequences of actions, we help form the basis for a good memory and logical thought. The opportunity to watch, help with and, therefore, experience, daily housekeeping, baking, gardening and so on helps create a solid foundation on which thought processes can be built. The more repetitive activities children experience, the easier it is for memory to develop. The joy of shared activities forms the golden memories of childhood, an important thought for us to bear in mind.

Memory is very important in relation to the child's own identity and world view. It helps confirm or change good or faulty perceptions. The child needs to be able to do this in order to adapt to her own experiences.

So we see that the child's thought processes are closely connected to sense experiences, actions, and language. The child perceives what is happening, and a wish to imitate is created together with a need to put the experiences into words.

An example would be baking. The adult is in the kitchen making buns; the child wants to participate and do what the adult is doing. The child watches how the bun is rolled out and tries to copy the same movements using a tiny piece of dough of her own. The adult sings a song or shares a rhyme or story suited to the actions, such as "Pat-a-cake, Pat-a-cake Baker's Man," and the child sings along. The buns are put on the tray and "put into the oven for baby and me." The child sees, tastes, touches, and listens to what happening around her. Words are attached to an object or an action. This plays a role in forming the foundation not only for language, but also for mathematics (counting of buns, measuring, weighing), logical thinking (experiencing a logical sequence of events), connecting objects with their function (buns for the meal) and so on.

Such experiences lead to independent concept formation, not connected with immediate sense perceptions. An example: Little Emma is standing in front of the fridge and says: "Emma wants juice, Emma wants juice." She cannot see the juice, but she can name it with words. She also knows that the juice is in the fridge and is using language to achieve what she wants.

We should remember, however, that childhood should be joyful. It is not learning that is important, but learning with joy: joy at being able to connect words and actions, and being able to express oneself and to repeat actions over and over. This joy leads to self-consciousness, which manifests around two-and-a-half to three years when the child says "I" about himself. Now the inner being comes into its own.

Most of us do not remember further back than three years old, and probably not even as far back as that, unless something dramatic happened during the first few years. The child's inner memory picture of a situation that occurred in the early years is heavily influenced by how the child experienced that situation, not necessarily corresponding to the outer facts. Siblings who experienced the same incident will often have totally different recollections, and the story is told in different ways. Both stories are the truth according to how the individual experienced the situation.

We don't know beforehand how children will perceive and experience events or spoken words. We do not know what their "reading" of a situation will be, or what feelings may be aroused as a result. What we should bear in mind is that we play a central role in how a child experiences any situation. Adults' inner relationship to themselves and their own feelings, generally, and especially within a situation being played out, will have a strong influence on the child's process of learning to think and feel as an independent human being.

When a child learns to walk and talk, he needs good role models to imitate. This situation is, of course, visible; we can see the imitation in the learned result. In the same way, although invisibly, the child needs good role models in order that good thoughts and feelings be aroused and stimulated. It's not quite so simple to see the imitation of our thought processes, even though we feel that it is at work, and may sometimes see it confirmed outwardly. The stronger the bond between child and adult, the greater the influence inner thoughts and feelings have on the child. In the first years of life the child is strongly attached to the people around him and to his surroundings. The more time a child spends with a beloved adult, the closer the connection between the two becomes.

As adults we can control our thoughts up to a point. We have the ability to develop an idea, for example. We follow the process from the initial thought, through feelings of excitement and enthusiasm, to taking active steps for making it a reality.

The opposite happens with the child. The child performs a spontaneous act without prior thought. The act triggers a good or not-so-good feeling, and this feeling makes the child think about the meaning or result of what happened. We can use this very important knowledge as the foundation for "teaching" the child during the first few years. Intellectual explanations, which are not based on experience, will totally pass them by. Children understand the *act* and the mood attached to it, rather than words expressing intellectual concepts.

With the awakening of self-consciousness around the age of three, the seed of independent thinking has been sown. Our role is to inspire creative, moral thought. We cannot teach the child how to think, either now or later, but we can be aware of our own thoughts and how we handle situations near the child. We teach through our own thoughts, actions, manners, and striving towards human morality. We do not impose, but show the way by ensuring that we are worthy of imitation. By doing this, we guide the child's path towards the development of independent thought. ♥

Chapter Three

The Adult's Responsibility Toward the Child Today

The Adult's Responsibility Toward the Child Today

What kind of environment is the child of today born into? What is the "spirit" of our time? What kind of effect does the environment have on our children?

We live in a world where the possibilities for change and betterment are more or less unlimited, especially in the Western world. Research and development in the fields of health and environment have contributed to an improved standard of living for many people, and physical, psychological, and social help is readily available. Here in Norway, and in most developed countries, the child encounters a materialistic, technological, and information-based society, where all basic needs are met for a majority of the population. But in spite of all the information and help available, there is a great deal of uncertainty and ignorance regarding what is needed for the good, healthy upbringing of children.

We do not know what the future holds, or what challenges, possibilities and obstacles will be encountered. Children need to be able to think creatively in order to meet all the new challenges to come. The basis for creative thinking is created during the first years of life, and we must carefully choose how the child uses this precious, brief time.

Many of us discover that we are short of time, even though the day is organized from morning to night. Not only are the weekdays organized, but we also plan our holidays and our spare time in detail. Time to do nothing, or time to digest and work with impressions and experiences, is limited for both children and adults today. Before and after kindergarten we are bombarded with offers of various activities we can do, and the children are affected whether they want to be or not. I don't think our children need that. One of the most important things for the child is to be left alone in peace, to have time to discover and wonder about the world and its possibilities.

Creating a peaceful and protected environment

During her formative years the child is like a big sense organ. Every impression in the environment is taken in by the child, who has no inner protection to reject what is harmful. This means that all influences go straight in without any "filter." Each impression or influence becomes part of the child, forming her both physically and psychologically. For parents and teachers this means that we have to be aware of which sense experiences and impressions we give the child. We have to consider whether our children are surrounded with what they need, or with things they should be protected from.

Little children in our age seem wide-awake and observant, but we must not be fooled into believing that they are more mature than they really are. During the first few years, all children need a protected and "dreamlike" existence, and maybe *especially* the ones that are extra "mature."

A growing number of children start kindergarten from one year of age—in some countries even earlier, at three to four months—and spend a long time away from home each day. Parents seek a place in the Waldorf kindergarten for infants because they work, or are busy with education, or they are single parents or working-from-home parents who wish for a Waldorf education for their children. And we as Waldorf teachers have to look at the parent's needs and consider what the alternative would be if we didn't take in their children.

In the Waldorf kindergarten, one of the most important objectives is to create a balance to the very hectic everyday life that most children experience. With us, the children are left in peace without too much "entertainment"—in other words, not too many adult-managed activities. We endeavor to create a peaceful and safe environment both in the surroundings and in our attitude. We want to give the child enough time to see and experience the surrounding world and the actions taken by adults. We let the child explore and discover his readiness for the next stage of development at his own tempo.

In this way, we take care of childhood, that precious time that passes by so very quickly. It demands that we be conscious of the choices we make on behalf of the child. We do not want to force or weigh children down intellectually. Nor should we subject the younger ones to activities which are specifically geared towards older children. These can be saved for later.

It is not the acquiring of factual knowledge that is the important goal in these early years. Young children need to be given the time and space to grow and cultivate and use their own initiative to explore the world and to master their own bodies. Our task is to provide this environment, and to protect them from too many stimuli or stressful impressions.

Recognizing the power of imitation

The newborn baby is combines outward helplessness with a wealth of hidden talent and the will to develop and grow. The inborn ability and desire to develop through imitation becomes stronger as the child feels her own independence and individuality.

All learning happens through imitating and copying in the first three years. During this time, imitation goes deeper than the spontaneous copying of actions, and does not apply only to outer life. It affects the whole child, in body, soul, and spirit. Everything a child absorbs has an effect on the physical body and the inner organs. Rudolf Steiner says: "Children imitate what happens in their physical environment, and in this process of imitation their physical organs are cast in the forms that thus become permanent."[9]

The ability to imitate, regardless of culture or society, is the child's most important tool for adapting to and absorbing impressions. Young children do not have the ability to understand or to protect themselves from the impressions which pour in through the senses. With the help of imitation, however, the child has the possibility to *answer* or respond to the impressions. Human development is dependent on outside and inside influences. There is constant interaction between the environment, the adults in that environment, and the child's individuality, which decides how and whom the child takes after. Imitation is central to this process.

Spontaneous imitation is observed early. The child sees something moving, which sets off an urge to move himself. The immediate stimulation becomes apparent when the child wants to copy the adult directly. Dad is baking bread and the child wants to bake, Mum is doing the dishes and the child wants to wash up. Mum wants to read the newspaper and the child wants to read the newspaper, Dad watches TV and the child wants to watch TV, and so on. As the child disengages from Mum and Dad and becomes more independent, imitation is experienced in an individual way through play.

---

9 Rudolf Steiner, *The Education of the Child*, p. 18.

Imitation happening on the spiritual level is more difficult to recognize. The child senses and imitates the inner reality of what and who we are as human beings. Our thoughts and feelings are imitated much in the same way as our actions are. Children, however, do not have the ability to understand or follow our thoughts and feelings; they only sense the ambience, mood, or tone in general.

It is often not easy to see which actions, feelings and thoughts children are imitating, but we should be aware that their capacity for imitation is always present. We can ask ourselves the question "What do we want the child to imitate?" We know that the child can sense what is behind our actions and words and that he also knows when we are *not* present in our actions and words. When we are baking bread, and lose ourselves in thought about what we are doing after work, or about a conversation we had yesterday, we notice that the child's concentration and excitement disappear as we disappear with our own thoughts. It is not enough that we use slow, distinct working processes if we are not authentic in our actions.

Rudolf Steiner said about the teacher's role:

Children take in all that we do, such as the ways we act and move. They are equally susceptible to our feelings and thoughts. They imitate us, and even if this is not outwardly noticeable, they nevertheless do this by developing tendencies for imitation that, through their organic soul forces, they press down into the physical organism. Therefore, education during these first two and a half years should be confined to the self-education of the adults in charge, who should think, feel, and act in a way that, when perceived by children, will cause them no harm.[10]

Some children manage to understand the impressions they receive through spontaneous imitation, using play and movement to do so. When children play it is possible for them to render harmless the things that they have found difficult or distressing. This will help them to master life as adults. Other impressions stay in the subconscious. We do not know, because we cannot see, what these impressions are, and we do not know their effect in the long run.

Imitation is transformed into a creative skill, allowing the child to participate in his own development. It is fantastic to watch the excitement and eagerness the child shows when wanting to imitate. This is a power that we should take care of and nurture.

---

10 Rudolf Steiner, *Soul Economy and Waldorf Education*, p. 110.

Being a role model

We adults are the role models for the child in all respects, whether through our actions, our feelings, our thoughts, or our attitudes. This is probably the most difficult task we have as parents. The stronger the bond is between child and adult, the stronger the adult influence will be. For instance, if mother or father crosses the road against a red light, it has a much bigger impact than when a stranger does the same. We should all should be aware of the fact that we are role models in every situation where there are children present.

The way in which we interact with children is heavily colored by our own upbringing. It is not an easy task to recognize this, but we should be aware of it and think through what we do. We have to know how and why we choose what we do together with our children.

So, what does the child actually need from the adult? He needs good examples to follow.

When the adult performs useful activities and is totally present in what she is doing, the child's sense perception stimulates imitation. Slow, steady movements that are predictable and happen in a particular sequence are easier for the child to follow. We see that sometimes the child will imitate the activity immediately and sometimes imitation occurs later. At home and in the kindergarten we see many examples of how the adult's actions are immediately copied.

In earlier times the child was surrounded by everyday activities such as cooking, washing, or mending. In Waldorf kindergartens we choose to do these activities, knowing how important it is for children to have real activities to imitate, as children have always had. A so-called "old-fashioned" family life with life-enhancing work done slowly and carefully provides opportunities for valuable imitation.

One of the main activities in the kindergarten which is shared by the children is cooking. As soon as an adult starts cutting the vegetables for soup, children quickly gather around wanting to help. Actions are performed in a calm and measured way, easy for the children to follow. Every child participates with varying degrees of expertise, speed, and ability according to age and stage of development. The older children get a knife and help to cut the vegetables, while the little ones are busy eating carrots or touching the vegetables. Regardless of what they are doing, they are taking part in the activity of transforming raw materials into soup. They experience the activity from start to finish, learning to understand the sequence, and connect what they see with their own activity. The more logically the working processes follow each other, the better the basis for later learning and understanding.

Another example is when an adult is washing up. It will not take long before some children will come to help. If we then leave them to do the dishwashing while we start making sandwiches, the dishwashing often becomes uninteresting and the children would rather make sandwiches. *Children want to be involved with the adult's work.*

Children can and want to be our little helpers from an early age. Even a little three-year-old benefits from the feeling of being useful. "Can you manage to carry the apples to the table?" or "Come, shall we carry the apples to the table together?" we say, giving the child the feeling that we trust that she can master the action by herself, and feel that she is valuable and taken seriously.

Our feelings, thoughts, and attitudes are much more difficult to control and be aware of than the things we do or say. We all have our personal problems and we also tend to be preoccupied with the huge conflicts taking place in the world. Children do not need that; they has more than enough to cope with in taking part in everyday activities. When two-year-old Anna takes a ball from John, this is a far more important issue to them than our problems or world conflicts. As teachers, we can try to leave our problems outside with our coats when we hang them up before entering the classroom or kindergarten. If we succeed in leaving our troubles behind before we start the day, it will be of great help to the child and to our co-workers. Nobody has taken the "coat"; it will still be hanging there when it's time to go home, but perhaps it will have become a little lighter during the course of the day.

Through our enthusiasm and genuine interest in what we do, we help create good relationships between children and adults. We may make mistakes, but our awareness of what we have done, and our efforts to do better next time, are perceived by the child. Children arrive in the world full of enthusiasm, desire, and determination to evolve, but rely on adults and the surroundings they provide for the rest. Both the physical being and spiritual essence must be protected and developed, according to the personality, characteristics, and possibilities of each child. Importantly, children experience our joy in being together and that we recognise their individuality.

It is said that the child learns more during the first three years than in the next thirty years. We are the child's teachers through our own attitudes. Everything that we want to teach a child, we must *do*. If we want him to develop good social skills, we must show interest, care, and wonder for others and the world. If we want the child to develop positive thought processes, we must think positively about others and ourselves. All of this contributes to the laying of a good

Providing opportunities to explore and practice new skills

When the child learns to grip, the foundation for writing is laid; when he learns to walk, the foundation is laid for cycling; when he learns to talk, the foundation is laid for learning Latin. Further mastering of knowledge depends on the learning process he has undergone as a child.[11]

The child from birth to three years is a little explorer, with boundless curiosity. The child crawls, toddles, and moves around the room. He "grabs" the world, wanting to discover, try out, make mistakes, and conquer the world on his own.

We bear this in mind when arranging the infant and toddler section of the kindergarten. Everything is placed so that the youngest children can develop according to their own abilities. Free play allows the best opportunity for them to develop at their own pace. Play gives children the freedom to choose for themselves what they wants to learn without the adult deciding and directing. We, the adults, are there, keeping a close watch while we continue with our work. We encourage the children to pull, push, shove, and lift the equipment we have selected for them. They are free to discover themselves, their abilities, and their place in interactions with the other children. Only when we notice something is too difficult or dangerous do we step in and help. At all times we consider what they can manage by themselves and when it is right for us to intervene and do what we can to help.

In our kindergarten, we had a little girl of eighteen months who was standing up in one of the high chairs and wanted to get down. She screamed in the hope that someone would lift her down. We could see that it would be very difficult for her to get down on her own without falling. How could we help her manage? We put a low bench near the chair, to make it easier to climb down. She understood immediately, and it did not take long before one foot was on the bench, and soon she had climbed down of her own accord! The smile and the look of pride that shone from her was sufficient reward for the child and us. "I managed by myself," she said without words.

There are many examples of this kind of helping children to help

---

11 William Stern, *Psychologie der frühe Kindheit*, p. 56. Translation by E. G. Paulsen.

themselves. Every time we succeed, the child has taken a further step in her own development and strengthened her own self-image. The child becomes more confident to explore and wants to do everything by herself. One of the first things a child says is "can do it myself," but often because we are pressed for time, we do not give children a chance to do it on their own. If we only could take the time to *see* their eagerness to dress themselves, even if they do not always succeed. We must give them enough time and something to strive for, and supply help instead of interruptions. How often have we watched a little one battling to put on sock or a shoe and the incredible pride and delight shown when the sock or shoe is in place!

During the first seven years of life, thoughts, feelings, and actions intermingle in a different way than in later years. As was mentioned earlier, normally an action happens spontaneously, followed by feelings brought about by what has been done, and then finally thoughts. The adult ability to direct actions out of a conscious thought process and understanding of consequences does not exist. The youngster is busy playing with a vase filled with flowers and water. Suddenly the vase falls on the floor and all the water runs out. The child reacts, maybe becomes afraid, and starts crying. The next time the vase filled with flowers is seen by the child, a connection will be made to the previous experience and a concept is formed. The more repeats of experiences, the more ideas are formed. ❦

## Chapter Four

The Child as a Sense Being

> *Predisposition to godhood is built into the human psyche. The way to this godhood—if one can speak of a "way" that never leads to a goal—is opened through the senses.*[12]   —Friedrich Schiller

When, following Rudolf Steiner, we say that the child is one big sense organ, what does that mean for the child? A sense organ receives many impressions and the body responds with movement. Some of the movements are visible, and others are not, as for example those that take place in the inner organs.

Consider an infant of three to five months. Not only are his eyes and ears following everything happening around him, but his whole body reacts. His arms and legs are moving without direction. When Mother or Father approaches, we see an increase in the movements. The recognition and joy when the baby senses the caregiver nearby provokes a strong reaction and the baby responds with his whole being.

The child is continuously surrounded by sensory experiences, not all of them good. One example with which we are all familiar is when we take the child along on a shopping spree. We have no way of protecting either the child or ourselves from the sights and sounds that bombard us in a shopping center. The child will receive more impressions than he can digest. Ask yourself how you feel after a day in a shopping center as opposed to a day on the mountains. In both places we have received impressions, but so very different. In the shopping center, we are assailed by impressions that exhaust us, and we are weary, not only physically, but also mentally. A day in the mountains also makes us

---

12 Friedrich Schiller, *Letters on the Aesthetic Education of Man*, Letter 11. Passage translated by E. G. Paulsen/L. Widmer. *Die Anlage zu der Gottheit trägt der Mensch unwidersprechbar in seiner Persönlichkeit in sich; der Weg zu der Gottheit, wenn man einen Weg nennen kann, was niemals zum Ziel führt, ist ihm aufgetan in den Sinnen.*

physically tired, but we get a great sense of well being.

There is a limit to what a child can absorb in one day. It is one thing to be physically exhausted, but what about the impressions that remain? Are they building up or breaking down the child's development? As adults, we have the option of distancing ourselves from sense experiences, because, as a rule, we understand what is happening. The child, however, does not have the same ability to distance himself from the surrounding impressions, nor to limit himself. Knowledge of how to rightly educate the young child must therefore be based in an understanding of the senses.

Rudolf Steiner has contributed enormously to this understanding. He described twelve senses, which he divided into three groups: the foundation senses, the middle senses, and the higher senses. All the senses are connected, but the focus of development differs at different ages. All the senses are there when the child is born, though some will remain hidden and in a kind of sleeping state until later. The senses help the child connect the inner world to the outer world, in a way particular to each individual child.

The senses of touch, life (or well-being), self-movement, and balance are the four lower senses, which we also call the foundation or the infrastructure for the child's development. These are closely connected to the physical body and the will. These senses are cared for and nurtured throughout life, but are especially important in the first seven-year period.

The senses of smell, taste, sight and warmth are the middle senses. They connect us to the world around us. These senses must obviously also be taken care of from the beginning, but they are of extra importance in the second seven-year period, from seven to fourteen.

The sense of thought, ego/individuality of other, language/speech and hearing are the higher senses that connect us to each other. These are the senses that must be reinforced in the third seven-year period, up to age twenty-one. The four lower senses form the foundation for the four higher senses:

Sense of touch	*Sense of ego/individuality of the other*
Sense of life	*Sense of thought*
Sense of self-movement	*Sense of language/speech*
Sense of balance	*Sense of hearing*

During the first seven-year period, the child uses will (volition) and self-initiated activity when adapting to sensory impressions. These are far stronger and more intensely experienced by a child than by an adult, as the child receives all impressions without a filter. It is thus very important that we control not only which impressions children receive, but how many, according to their age and stage of development.

The sense of touch

The skin, our largest sense organ, is the organ for the sense of touch. It is closely linked to the sense of safety and well-being and perhaps the most important sense for the child under three.

The book *Baby Massage* refers to investigations done in 1977, which show that positive touch, in addition to daily care, is very important for growth and the development of language and social skills.[13] Through experience, we have learned that positive touch makes the child feel safe and loved.

Even as a fetus moving in the womb, the baby experiences touch. At this stage it is vague, as the temperature for mother and baby is the same. This changes when the baby comes into the world and is met by light and air, along with the touch of the caregiver and of clothing. For most newborn babies, the first experience of touch is a positive one. Carefully and lovingly, she is put on her mother's breast and feels the warmth of her skin. Through the tender touch of her parents' hands, the feeling of safety is given. The child perceives not only physical touch, but also the state of mind of the people touching her. Through touching herself and others, the child awakens and becomes aware of her own body. By sensing the difference between her own body and another object, she begins to know whether something is cold, warm, soft, wet or dry.

The child starts out in life by meeting boundaries: I am here, out there is the world. She experiences herself not only through other living beings but also through things and objects. When a child touches a table, she realizes that here is the border between the hand and the table.

The sense of touch is closely connected to the sense of ego, which is still in a sleeping mode. Slowly, as self-consciousness awakes, the child's own identity emerges. When touched by another, the child becomes more aware of herself and her individuality. She senses that it is this individuality that is being "touched." The sense of ego, which will awaken later, has to do with sensing the individuality of another being.

---

13 Nicki Bainbridge and Alan Heath, *Baby Massage*, p. 45.

In the relationship between adult and child touch is important—not only physical touch. The underlying attitudes and intentions of the adult are just as meaningful as the sense-perceptible qualities, such as whether our hands are warm or cold. The child picks up these intentions just as strongly as the physical touching itself. Touching an infant normally happens in a tender and careful manner, as if we are afraid to hurt or damage this little wonder. Even our voices become soft and subdued around a newborn. These are qualities and ways of being that we as adults must preserve, not only during the first few months, but also throughout childhood. A three-year old also needs this sensitivity and gentleness, even through the turbulent tantrum period—in fact especially then!

Simply being close to another person is another kind of touch. We can keep a hand near a person without direct touch, yet still "feel" him or her. The touch sense transcends the physical body and our skin.

Everyday acts of loving physical care and nurturing strengthen and foster the touch sense, both at home and in the kindergarten. Some happen during normal routines and the daily rhythm, while others happen spontaneously. We activate the sense of touch every time we put a child to bed, pick him up again when he awakes, or hold him when he is sad and in need of help and comfort. While caring for the child, we can massage the feet or hands while singing or reciting a little verse. This does not have to last long, but it helps to strengthen a feeling of safety and well-being. We also need to give children the opportunity to climb onto a lap just for a cuddle.

In the kindergarten, we have a small washbasin placed low enough for the children to be able to wash their hands with a little help from an adult. The touch of their own hands, the adult's hands, and the running water promotes gales of mirth. This activity needs lots of time. The hands are then dried and we sit down at the table. A small drop of oil is put in the hands while we sing or speak a rhyme. Everyone notices the aroma of the oil and feels the softness of the hands, and some even feel their neighbor's hands. Some children love to feel the touch of another person rubbing in the oil, while others prefer to rub the oil into their own hands. Sometimes we have children who do not want oil on their hands, nor to be touched, and we respect this. These little encounters are very important to the child's development.

A game most children enjoy is to lie on the floor and hide their heads while we sing the song "When the troll mother has laid her eleven little trolls to bed," and softly and carefully touch them on their backs. Most enjoy it. Sometimes this is the best way of touching someone who is not normally keen to be touched, but perhaps needs it more than most. We have to be cautious and respectful of each child. If we manage to carefully observe every child, they will let us know *what* they need and *when*.

The sense of life

The sense of life is a thread throughout all the senses. It tells us if we are hungry, tired, or not feeling well. It alerts us to the state of our body and its inner organs, glands, nerves, digestive processes, and so on. The child discovers what is happening in the body through the life sense. Some children experience the life sense stronger than others and can point out where their body hurts, whereas others can only express pain, but not where it is located. Typically, the child under three is living as one with its environment; he does not separate himself from the surroundings. Little Henry hits his leg on the edge of the table and when the adult asks where he has hurt himself, Henry will point to the table and not to his leg.

Small children let us know something is wrong through their body language and behavior. Even though they cannot use language to inform us of what is wrong, they express their distress through tears or other signals. Their happiness is great when finally their parents understand what they want, be it food or a clean diaper. The sense of life is not only connected to well-being but also to pain. It serves as a warning system for the body and the child's well-being. Pain takes the focus away from the joy of life, but as soon as the pain goes away, the "joie de vivre" returns. As long as we have happy children around us, the sense of life is usually in balance.

In the kindergarten and in the home, the sense of life is cared for in many ways. A close and caring adult, providing safety and security, strengthens the life sense and quality of life. We can also nurture the child's sense of life by creating good habits and rhythms. Good habits are formed through repetition over a long period of time. For example, the children put on slippers before they go into the playroom, and everybody washes their hands before eating. Good habits create a sense of safety and predictability that in turn create harmony in the child's day. Set times for meals, washing, sleeping, and play are another prerequisite for the child's well-being.

The sense of self-movement

Child is synonymous with *movement*. Most healthy children are constantly moving, which is as it should be. Children are always moving unless they are eating, sleeping, or ill.

The sense of self-movement lets us know whether the body is quiet or moving. We become conscious of our body through our own movements. Together with the sense of touch and the sense of life, movement begins at the fetal stage. A pregnant woman can feel when the child moves and kicks. After birth the sense of self-movement becomes ever more noticeable as the child "lives into" her own body. The movement of an infant is chaotic and without direction in the beginning, although sometimes wilful actions take place on an unconscious level. Through the impulses received from the world around it, the child is stimulated to copy actions. Every little movement registers. As the muscles are used, the child first has an awareness of their contraction and and relaxation. From the day the child stands upright and takes her first step, her life is filled with her own actions and movements. Movement is discovered as an inner experience when the child sees something in motion and follows it. The child controls her own motion by inner willpower, by adapting her own response to what she experiences.

From the crawling stage through learning to walk, most children are in constant motion. The eagerness displayed in discovering and controlling one's own body is unique to that age. In a relatively short time and with tremendous effort, the child succeeds in taking her first steps. Once more, we repeat that the child needs this time to battle on her own without help. The adult's job is to create a safe environment so the child can manage on her own.

The child's own sense of movement and the ability to use her body will have an effect on how the child will control her body and on how she will develop physically. By giving a child the opportunity to perform all kinds of movements, we help to give her self-control of the body, which is very important for her self-esteem and self-image.

In the kindergarten, in the area for the little ones, we use many songs, rhymes, and jingles, all of which help stimulate movement. The adult sits down on a carpet and sings a song accompanied by simple movements. It does not take long before children join in, some sitting next to the adult and some on the adult's lap. A "good morning" song is sung, and all the children are mentioned by name, while they are gently stroked on the arm or back. Most children love to sing and often sit down even before the adult does when the time is near for this activity. Some children may prefer to sit under the table and watch, some run away, and others want to do something else. They are allowed to do this at this age. We need patience to trust that the child will come when he is ready, and will participate at his own pace without being forced. After a while, we get to know the children so well that we recognize when a child runs away simply because he wants to be fetched by the adult. We have to consider that the child might be in need of something, and that we might have to include or cater for that need. The rub-off effect is of course great at this age, and we need to keep an awareness of when someone really needs to be fetched and when we must look for other reasons.

We get great enjoyment from singing and moving with the children, but most importantly movement is stimulated through our actions. The child joins us, and soon the activity becomes what the child personally chooses to do.

Children need to explore without too much help from adults. They need time, not only to learn but to become comfortable with a newly learned activity. The adult, who stays close by all the time, can give encouragement and help if necessary, or if it seems that the child is stuck and needs to be guided to overcome the challenge. The pleasure of succeeding on his own is very valuable for the child.

During the free play period, children have the possibility for all sorts of movements, but this depends to a great extent on the physical environment. Do the children have enough room to move? What about toys and equipment? We need tables, benches, chairs, and baskets that can be moved, pulled, pushed, climbed on, and used for various operations that children can manage on their own. Apart from the physical environment, it is important that the adult be there to inspire play and encourage movement.

The sense of balance

Through sensing our equilibrium, we know if we are in balance—physically, but also psychologically. We overcome the pull of gravity when we stand upright, and our sense of balance keeps us from falling over. It tells us our position in space and how to carry ourselves when we move in any direction. The outer framework (e.g. the walls of a room) helps us to keep our balance; we need something to which we can anchor ourselves. As long as we remain on a floor or ground that remains steady, we do not have a problem. However, as soon as this ground starts moving, for example in a boat, our consciousness increases in proportion to the effort required to keep our balance. As soon as we are back on land and everything is back to normal, we regain our balance again and no longer have to be conscious of maintaining it.

The upright position is unique to the human being and is connected to the ego or I. We experience the self when we are upright and take a step. The sense of balance makes a connection between the exterior ground on which we stand and the inner self.

Here is an example from the youngest kindergarten group that demonstrates the connection between balance and the dawn of self-awareness. It was spring and three girls who are moving up to the next level (age three to six) in the kindergarten in autumn were playing together.

One of the girls climbed on one of the high stools we use at meals and stood upright. She kept her balance while moving around, and sang: "I am on top, I am on top." This was repeated several times and she managed to keep her balance while singing. The next girl dragged a chair next to the first one, climbed up and sang the same words, "I am on top, I am on top." A third little girl did the same, climbing up and joining the choir. They kept going for a while, laughing and having fun, singing the same song. Suddenly there was a variant: one of the girls started singing "WE are on top," and after a while they all sang "WE ARE ON TOP."

What an experience for these three, especially the one who discovered that *I* am here and *we* are together. They did it without any interference from an adult. Their new knowledge was not connected to the danger that they might fall off the chairs. Preventing the latter was our responsibility; the former was the task of the child.

Physiologically, we rely on three fluid-filled canals in the inner ear as the organs of the sense of balance. If they are damaged, equilibrium is affected. These physical organs must be in order, working together with our own will and ego, to keep us in balance.

At the moment that an infant tries to lift his head and keep it up, the sense of balance is activated. This is the start of the child's great and continuous effort towards getting up and taking his first steps. If we observe children during this phase, we will see how they use their arms to balance. When they try to run, it looks as though they are balancing on a plank, with arms straight out to the sides.

Children experience great satisfaction in the ability to keep the body in balance, and during the course of a day there are many opportunities for a little child to practice it, both at home and in the kindergarten. We can arrange the surroundings to be favorable for such practice. Providing solid benches, tables, or stools that can be used for climbing and balancing on encourages children to be active. Wooden bricks in various sizes and forms can be used for building and balancing. How tall can a tower of blocks be? How many blocks can I put on top of each other before they crash down? If the opportunities are there, the child will experiment by himself.

There is never just one sense being used, and there are usually several at the same time. The sense of movement, the sense of sight, and the sense of balance are interdependent. The child must be able to co-ordinate these senses. As long as we are moving around and can see where we are going, we are fine. But if we close our eyes, we quickly lose balance and have to use extra concentration to regain steadiness. Little children usually fall down if they close their eyes while moving.

Conclusion

Connecting to the world and forming new concepts is a process that will continue through life. Different forces are used depending on where the child is developmentally. All the senses used during the first years are connected to the body. Later we will see how this develops on the soul and spiritual level. If the child experiences logical actions in the first years, a base is laid for logical thinking later on in life.

We have taken as a starting point people who have the possibility of developing all their senses. However, when individuals have dysfunctional sense organs, often other senses will compensate for the loss. Some have become famous for their unusual abilities and gifts. One example is Jacques Lusseyran, who lost his sight at the age of eight but developed his sense of hearing to the point that he could tell whether someone told the truth or not. He also was able to directly sense another person's soul quality without seeing him or her. He said, "By losing the ability to see, I gained the capacity to pay attention, something I feel everybody can do, but has lost the ability."[14]

This example, along with many others—Helen Keller and Stephen Hawkins are two others that come to mind—can help us not to take our senses for granted. We should strive to cultivate all the capacities that children bring with them, and not allow them to be dulled or lost through inattention. This begins in the earliest years when we rightly appreciate and educate the foundational senses. ♡

---

14 Jacques Lusseyran, *Zwei Vortrage in Zurich*, p. 29. Passage translated by E. G. Paulsen.

Chapter Five

Rhythm and Time in the Child's Daily Routine

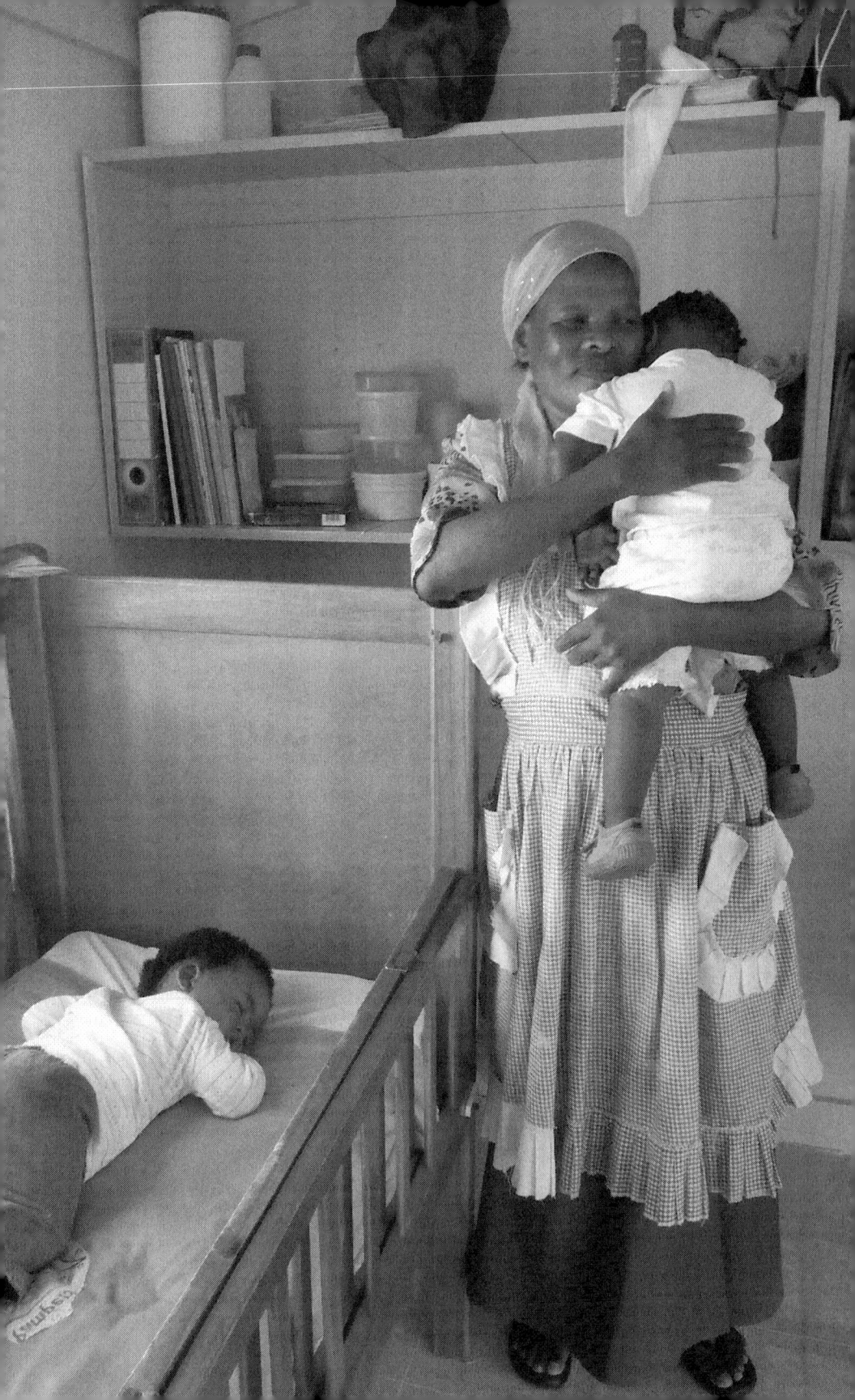

Rhythm (from Greek *rhythmos*, any regular recurring motion, symmetry) is a "movement marked by the regulated succession of strong and weak elements, or of opposite or different conditions."[15]

Rhythm is an important aid to the upbringing of the growing child, and indeed is a necessity for our lives as human beings. It is given to us by nature; we find it everywhere where there is life and growth. Rhythm is about cadence and tempo, regularity and measure. We experience it whenever there is alternation between two polarities. These alternations can be fluid and mobile at the same time that they follow a definite sequence and order, which is continually repeated. For example, think of water drops falling from the roof or a water tap dripping.

In our daily lives, rhythm is largely about expansion and contraction. We experience how day expands our vision and our activity, and night brings us back home to rest. In the change of seasons we can see the alternating expansion and contraction of the earth, its breathing in in winter and out in summer.

We can compare rhythm in nature with the rhythm in our physical body. We can look at a brook where the water is in movement. The water itself has no inherent rhythm, but as it trickles and flows downwards it creates one. The water's movement depends on what it meets on its journey: stones, twigs, and other objects contribute to the way the water will flow, but the flow pattern that we see is repeated again and again and never ends. If we put a stone in the brook or a large branch, the water will still continue flowing, but will find new ways to do so.

---

15 *The Compact Edition of the Oxford English Dictionary, II*, p. 2537.

In us, rhythmic movement is experienced in our breathing and blood circulation. The same rhythm is maintained as long as there is no interference from outside. However, as soon as something happens to us, whether to body, soul, or spirit, our breathing and blood circulation is affected. Just as the movement of the brook is influenced by outer conditions, so is the child affected by outside happenings.

The earthly rhythms of living beings are interwoven with universal cosmic rhythms. The moon and sun have their own rhythm connected to week, month and year. Our planet needs twenty-four hours to turn on its own axis, which creates the alternation of day and night that affects every living being on earth. At the same time each individual has its own unique rhythm. Human beings have not only physical rhythms, but also soul and spiritual rhythms that are at work throughout our lives. Understanding the importance of rhythm helps us grasp the significance of bringing it into the child's life.

The significance of rhythm in the child's development

We no longer live according to nature's rhythms as our ancestors did. Science and technology have revolutionized our everyday lives and transformed the way we live. In place of the experience of natural dark and light, we press a button and there is light, even if it is in the middle of the night. We use artificial light and warmth to grow flowers and plants. We also interfere in people's lives by using chemical medicines that affect blood circulation and breathing.

Nevertheless, we must not forget that we still are subject to nature's rhythm. We cannot get the sun to rise in the evening or prevent plants from turning toward the light; it is the law of nature that the sun will rise in the morning and that plants will reach out toward the sun. The rhythm in nature still affects us and our development. We must take this into account in the upbringing of our children, keeping it in mind as we shape our daily routine.

Everything that happens in and around a child affects the body's rhythm. Regularity in everyday life helps strengthen the child's growth and progress. An everyday life that changes from day to day is disturbing to the child. Predictability, on the other hand, gives a sense of safety.

We should be aware that the rhythm in children's everyday lives has changed radically in the last fifty years, generally becoming less regular and predictable. For example, rather than staying in one place, the child of today has often moved or been abroad several times before starting school.

Rhythm and Time in the Child's Daily Routine

The child comes into the world from a protected time in the womb where she has shared the mother's rhythm during pregnancy. From birth, the infant starts to experience living at her *own* pace. She takes her first breath, breathing in, breathing out. Initially the breath is uneven, but after a while, it acquires its own individual rhythm. Influences from outside, whether they are movements in the room, sounds, or feelings of hunger, discomfort, or happiness, will all have an effect on the child's breathing. Each time the child is fed, wakes up, or goes to sleep, it leaves an imprint on the daily rhythm.

In the beginning after birth, the mother's rhythm is still a strong influence. Later on, the child finds her own tempo. This is affected by cultural practices. In Africa, where it's common to carry the infant on the back, the child experiences the mother's rhythm as she moves and works. Children who are rocked in a cradle have another experience of rhythm. Many parents tell us that those children who have been rocked as infants become calmer and more amicable.

Little children need a more rhythmic, regulated day than adults do. It is easier for them to orientate themselves when they know what is going to happen. In contrast to us adults, children experience just as much excitement with the familiar as they do with the unknown.

To create a good rhythm for a child takes a great deal of time and patience. It is only possible if we repeat the same thing over and over again, every day, for a long period of time. Only then will it be regular enough to influence the child positively.

In earlier times, children experienced rhythm more strongly through the manual work of those around them. Mothers did laundry by rubbing clothes on the washboard, or kneaded bread by hand. Cutting grain with a sickle was another activity with recurring movements. Today there are not many children who experience these rhythmical movements, especially in the Western world. We really do not wish to go back to the times without mechanical aids; however, we can see the importance of learning how people performed these tasks. Children do not have the possibility to observe the working process when it is done by machines. If we believe that the power of imitation is the child's tool for learning, it is important that the child have something to imitate. It's much easier to imitate an adult washing up than a dishwasher that does the same job!

All regular processes affect the child. Breathing, nerves, and blood circulation are affected, and the consequence is either calming or disturbing. Children are happy and content if their world is calm and mostly regular. This can have a calming effect on restless or nervous youngsters. It creates a safe and predictable environment.

In the Waldorf kindergarten, we alternate between ordered activities on the one hand and free play on the other. This gives the child the possibility of a rhythmic "breathing" during the kindergarten day. When the child has to concentrate, that is an "in" breath. Activities prepared and structured by adults demand concentration within given limits. When a child plays by himself, there is also deep concentration—but the child sets the limits, and because it is not directed from outside, it is an "out" breath. The alternation between directed and free activities gives the child space for rhythmic "in-breathing" and "out-breathing." We clearly see this when we tell a fairy tale or a little story. Children absorb the words with full concentration; it almost seems as if they are holding their breath. When the story is finished, we see how they expel the breath.

A child's daily routine needs to contain both breathing polarities in alternation, organized rhythmically by the adult caregivers. The child has more than enough to handle in performing his daily tasks, and at the same time exploring his own dexterity, without uncertainty being added to the mix.

The rhythm in everyday life is important, but it is also important to make room for the spontaneous. We can allow ourselves that, once we have created a solid everyday routine. It is not little exceptions that disturb the routine, but continuous changes. A few exceptions spice up the day, while the routine gives stability and safety. When we are on holiday or have a day off, we break the normal routine. We enjoy lazy mornings without an alarm clock telling us to get up. Sometimes we turn the day upside down. This can be exciting for a while, but eventually most of us long for the known routine. We like to have some order in our lives. For the little child this is of paramount importance. Children can behave spontaneously, but are happiest in a routine provided by adults.

Taking time for children

Children spell love: T-I-M-E
—Dr Anthony P. Witham

We all have our mechanical helpers, which should give us more time because they handle many of our daily chores. However, we still run out of time and do not get everything done. We often feel that "if I could only get this thing done, everything would be so much better." Nevertheless, as soon as we complete one task, another appears.

We can take control of our time again by having a greater awareness of what we actually want and need to do. We can choose to have less activity during the day and make room for quietness, which is something we all need. All of us, children and adults, need enough time and space for ourselves.

The age of each particular child, his stage of development, and his personality give us a hint as to what he needs, especially during the first three years. That is the period when children acquire many skills in a short span of time. During these years, they not only learn skills, but also need to practice what they have learned. They need repetition and time to practice. We tend to forget that when a child has learned something new, he needs time to learn, adapt, and repeat that skill before hurriedly moving on to the next item.

Our children are our teachers when it comes to upbringing. Rudolf Steiner maintains by reading the child's nature, you will know what he needs. In his book *The Education of the Child* he speaks of educators of the future who will observe children deeply:

> They will invent no programs, but read from them [the children] what is already there. What they read becomes in a certain sense the program itself, for it bears within it the essence of development. For this very reason a spiritual-scientific insight into the being of humankind must provide the most fruitful and most practical means for the solution of the questions of modern life.[16]

That means that we, as educators, must learn to listen to and observe each child during each phase. This will give us the knowledge we need to help the child in his development. For the little ones it is obvious what they want and need: constant repetition of actions and words. Everyone who works with children of this age hears constantly, "Do that one more time," and "Tell us again."

Young children want to spend time with adults on a daily basis, and participate in various daily chores. They do not look for "entertainment" or wish to be kept busy with all sorts of activities. It is for our own convenience that we put a child in front of the television while we are cooking supper. I believe that if children could choose, they would choose the company of an adult unless they have acquired other habits.

We also need to give children enough time to adapt to all the

---

16 Rudolf Steiner, *The Education of the Child*, p. 4.

new impressions that bombard them. The experiences that a child is exposed to during a normal day trigger different images in the brain and contribute to the foundation for future thoughts. The more logical actions that happen in the day, the more logical the thoughts will be that are formed later. In addition, the more children perceive and understand through their own actions, the easier it will become to understand cause and effect when they are older. Children need to feel, observe, and do things themselves. We need to give them space, peace, and enough time to do just that. All healthy progress, growth, and maturation needs time.

Emmi Pikler writes in her book *Lass Mir Zeit* ("Give Me Time") how important it is that we observe the child and create the right conditions for independent movements and actions from birth. Having studied young children over many years, she describes the skills they have for movement, the progression during the first years, and how those skills are used. The book's title says it all! With toddlers, especially, we have to have enough time for what we want to do and be *present* in what we do. In that way the child has the opportunity to be deeply focused in the activity, and this will later give a further understanding of what is happening. Today, when most things happen at the speed of lightning, it is very important that we give children—and ourselves—time.

The consciousness of time is closely connected to the maturation of the brain, which continues through life. At birth the brain surface begins to mature, so that the brain cells can start functioning. This happens as sense impressions from outside are absorbed and adapted by the child. At the beginning, babies have no conception of time. They live in the present, and time is connected to specific events. Only later will time be something the child understands as a concept. A first experience of time comes about when something is repeated and is connected to a sense experience of touch, sound, smell, and taste. An infant cries because she is hungry. When the mother puts the child to her breast and the baby feels the mother's skin, the cries change to "happy" sounds because she knows that milk is coming soon. This is the beginning of understanding the concept of time.

In general, timing is the key to healthy eating habits. When a youngster is hungry and wants food we do not wait hours or days before giving him the food she needs. We know that if we waited too long, the child would develop problems with the digestive system and might get stomach cramps. Digestion is connected to the type of nutrition the child receives and to regular feeding intervals. In the Waldorf kindergarten we place an enormous amount of importance on healthy and nutritious food, mainly biodynamic and natural unprocessed foodstuffs, and meals are at set times.

The importance of time is not so obvious when it comes to soul nourishment. Most children let us know when they need our attention, be it with words, body language, or behavior. We do not always have time there and then, and we may ask the child to wait a little while. Sometimes a long time passes before we attend to the child, or we forget that she has tried to make contact. We do not always recognize the problems or consequences that can follow when the spirit does not receive the nourishment it needs at the right moment. The implications of that could show up later in adult life.

Anna Tardos, the daughter of Emmi Pikler, gave a lecture about children at an International Kindergarten Meeting in Belgium in 2000. She made a strong impression on the audience when she spoke about and demonstrated the phenomenon of time. When she sat, she sat. When she stood up, she stood up. She took a lot of time performing these actions and every movement was slow and obvious. We experienced this as a movie in slow motion. Her point was that we have to learn to use more time in everything we do, and do one thing at a time. At home, this is not always possible, but as educators and workers in a kindergarten, we have the opportunity and obligation to give the time the child needs, and create space so that it can be possible. We need to learn the value of slowness and presence, especially for children. In today's society in the Western world, time may be the most valuable commodity we can give children.

Creating a good daily routine

Parents often feel they do not have enough time for their children. We also experience this in the kindergarten even though our objective is to have enough time. Much has to be done to cover basic needs. The daily routine must be planned based on individual needs and the amount of time considered necessary.

During the first seven-year period, we work with imitation. That means we have to look at ourselves as role models and ask ourselves how we work with rhythm in our own lives. Do we have enough time for an out-breath and rest? Do we exhaust ourselves or burn out coping with daily chores? If that is the case, we should make room for "little pockets" of time, whether for art, meditation, or just a quiet moment. It creates a counterbalance that helps us, and in turn affects the child.

In the kindergarten in the infant/toddler group, we put an emphasis on a good daily routine with meal times, care, sleep, and play. In addition to that, we wash clothes, iron, dust, water plants and do other tasks when we have time. The children need good activities to copy and enough time to absorb them. That is why we choose few activities and allow ourselves plenty of time to do them.

Meals are prepared with the help of the children. Sometimes they are actively involved, while at other times they sit and watch. We make a point of working slowly enough for them to follow the process. They see how the apple is peeled and cut into pieces, or how we mix flour, yeast, and water when baking. They have the opportunity to follow our movements in everything we do. The slower our movements are, the easier they are for them to understand.

Through repeating various chores each day, we create good habits and a safe setting for the children. The way in which each child perceives what is happening and the way in which he will emulate the adult is an individual act. It all depends on the children's own innate abilities and personality and what opportunities they have. With children under three, it is not important to fill the day with too many different activities. At this age they have enough to do with exploring their own abilities and surroundings. They need adults who look after them, giving help where it is needed, while busy doing useful household work. Through this, the child experiences safety and predictability. Unforeseen occurrences do happen in this group, and this is something we need to take into account. Diapers need changing, a nose needs wiping, somebody fell, or someone is crying. Conflict happens, and time is needed for comfort and coaxing before we can resume normal activities.

The rhythm in this group must be primarily to accommodate the children, but it must also be good for the adults. If the children are happy, the adults are content. If the adults are happy, the children flourish. To create a happy day, the prerequisite is that we have enough time. That is reflected in everything we do.

A good daily routine is of paramount importance, especially in autumn when children enter the kindergarten for the first time. There are lots of things for the children to get used to and many new experiences during the course of a day. The proceedings are, for the most part, the same things that happen at home within the family: play, meals, singing, and movement.

A day in the kindergarten

Here is an example of a day in the kindergarten, *one* way of doing it. The model is the toddler group in our kindergarten in Norway, with ten children ages one to three.

7:30	The children arrive and play freely while breakfast is being prepared
8:00	Breakfast
8:30	Free play
10:15	We wash our hands, and have singing and movement in a "ring"
10:30	Lunch
11:00–2:00	Care (changing diapers, preparing for sleep), followed by nap
on waking	Small fruit meal and drink, time depending when children wake up, accompanied by care (diapers, dressing)
1:30–3:00	Free play, outside or inside, depending on season and weather. Some children go home between 2:00 and 3:00.
2:30	Meal for afternoon children
3:30	Free play, or a quiet time, e.g. "reading" a book
4:15	Kindergarten closes

To provide one example from our kindergarten, we will follow two-year-old Pia during a regular day. Pia is the second of three siblings. An older sister is in another section of the kindergarten and the youngest brother is still at home.

It is eight o'clock and Pia arrives with her sister and mother. A joyful Pia comes through the door and runs straight away to her place in the locker room, sits down and starts taking off her shoes. She wants to put on her slippers by herself and she tries, but needs a little help from her mother before they are on comfortably. Now Pia is ready to go in. The educator carefully opens the door to the main room where breakfast is being served. Mum stands in the doorway and says goodbye. Pia first looks into the room before she turns around to her mother and says "cuddle." Mum gets a cuddle and Pia runs to the table.

At mealtimes, the children have their fixed places. They sit in high chairs around the table. The ones who are able to climb up have permission to do so.

Pia climbs up by herself, but needs a little help to get into the chair.

Once most of the children are in place, we light the candle and everybody sings: "The soil nurtures the little seed; the sun ripens the grain to bread. Dear sun and dear earth, thank you for the gifts on our table.

Bless the food." We all hold hands (this is voluntary) and then we start eating.

> Pia wants crispbread, and with a little help from the adult, she gets butter and cheese on her piece and starts eating. Pia can manage two slices of crispbread or a slice of regular bread for breakfast. Pia enjoys her food, frequently puts a hand on her neighbour, and often has lots to say.

After breakfast, while we tidy up, is the time for free play.

> Pia climbs down from the chair, but needs a little help to get right down onto the floor. She runs to the adult and asks for a dishcloth; she wants to help clean the table. This takes a while and the dishcloth lands on the floor. Then she is in the corner with the dolls, where she has found a knotted doll that she carries around with her. She spots Jacob who has a little cat. Suddenly she really wants that cat. She lets go of the doll and takes the cat from Jacob. This results in screaming and objections. Pia looks impervious and holds on tight. The adults want to help. They find another cat, give it to Pia and together they return the cat to Jacob. It is not quite what Pia wanted, as she'd rather have the cat that Jacob had, so after a bit of coaxing Jacob accepts the new cat and Pia gets to keep the one she wanted. Big smile, and a few seconds pass before Pia returns the cat to Jacob. Now he has two cats and Pia has already moved on to something else. Free play among the little ones is constantly changing; sometimes it's not possible to follow all the details.

When playtime is over, the adults tidy up before opening the door to the bathroom where everyone has to wash hands.

> Pia has found a bag that she has filled with blocks. She is sitting on the floor engrossed in emptying the bag. Then she realizes that the door is open. She leaves the bag and runs into the bathroom to wash her hands. Someone is already standing at the basin. She wants to push him away, but is stopped by the adult. She protests a bit, but accepts having to wait for her turn. At the basin, she lets the water run across her hands and wants to linger there, but there are others waiting behind her. She gets help with drying her hands, then runs into the room again and sits down on the carpet.

One educator helps with the washing of hands and another sits down on the floor to gather the children for song and play, while the third makes sure we have all we need for the meal.

Pia wants to sit close to one of the adults. If someone is already sitting there, she tries to sneak in between so that she is sitting alongside an adult or on the lap. Sometimes this works, but at other times she has to find another place. Most of the time Pia participates in singing, rhymes, and jingles, but at other times it is more fun to hide under the table or run around a bit.

Depending on the child and the situation, we bring the children back to the group, or we let them be and they come back when are they ready. Most of them participate in all the songs and enjoy the repetition. Often we sing the same songs throughout the year. The latest one is "We are traveling to Eating land" and all the children are mentioned by name in the song.

Pia is one of the first to run to the table and sit down. She would prefer to climb up by herself, but needs a little helping hand.

When everyone is in place, an adult walks around and puts a drop of oil (lemon or lavender oil) in the children's hands, while we recite a verse. We massage the oil into the hands, feeling the warmth and smelling the wonderful fragrance and sometimes touching each other's hands.

Pia sits and waits for the oil; she loves the fragrance and warm hands of the adult. She would really like to massage the hands of Preben, who is sitting next to her, but he will not allow it.

The children are wearing large bibs. The candle on the table is lit. We sing the same song we sang at breakfast, "The soil nurtures the little seed." Each child receives a plate of food according to the daily menu and we start eating. We try to keep a peaceful mood at the table, so the adults do not talk more than necessary. There is generally a little prattle going on, as someone is usually repeating and practicing new words just learned.

Pia loves to natter, even though she does not have all the words to express her meaning. However, through her body language and mimicry she succeeds in expressing most things.

Not everyone finishes eating at the same time, but we close off the meal with a verse that expresses, "Thank you for the food, it was very good and we are all satisfied." The children who want to will hold hands. After the meal, they are all cared for before having a nap. This is the time of day where each child gets his or her own time with the adult. One by one, they are taken into the baby care room for a diaper change before a nap. The parents decide whether the child should sleep outside in a pram or inside in a bed.

We try to use as much time as we can for this part of the day. Rhymes, jingles, and songs are used when removing the socks and finding all the toes, or getting the arms through the pullover. If there is time, we use a little oil for massaging legs or arms, which helps foster a sense of well-being and calm before falling asleep.

> Pia sleeps inside and she happily follows the adult to the care room to get a clean diaper before lying down. Again, she wants to climb up to the washbasin by herself, which she manages most of the time. With a little help, she gets ready and finds a clean diaper on the shelf. The diaper is changed, but before the long pants are put on, we play a little game with her toes, saying Tip, Tip, Tip every time we touch one of them. We could repeat that over and over again and she would never get tired of it, but now she must sleep.

Each child has a favorite song, which we will sing at this time. Some want the same song twice; others want two different songs or maybe even three different ones. A children's harp tuned to the pentatonic scale D–E–G–A–B–D–E will calm the children and help them sleep. The soft and tender tones of the harp are soporific. Some enjoy being tucked in, while others are happy with a touch on the cheek; others again need a bear hug before settling down. The needs of the individual children vary and as we get to know each and every one, we come to understand them. It is very important that the children bring their own familiar bedding from home, or at least a scarf from Mum or a T-shirt from Dad, especially in the beginning. The smell of home can create a feeling of safety and help to make sleep easier.

> Pia has two songs that she wants to hear before going to sleep, "Hum to me, Mummy" and "My guardian angel." Both songs are repeated a couple of times before she gets a cuddle and is then tucked in. She falls asleep easily. Sometimes we need to play on the harp a little, but as a rule, she falls asleep quickly.

Waking up is just as important as falling asleep. Again, we need time for each of the children, in order that they enter peacefully into our world again. They meet us in individual ways when they wake up. Some children are wide-awake straight away and stand up shouting; others stay under the covers and need a long time to waken. The way that we interact with them at this point will often determine the rest of the day. As adults, we feel very privileged to be part of this segment of the child's life, when they come from a deep sleep to an awakened state. Sometimes it is necessary to have children on our laps for a while, to give them enough time to wake up. A touch on the cheek or stroking the back makes it easier for them. One way of "waking" the child is through songs or fingerplays that are connected to rhymes and jingles.

> Pia normally sleeps one to two hours every day and she wakes up as peacefully as she falls asleep. Happy as a little bird, she often stands up in the bed waiting to be picked up. She does not need much time before she is ready to be dressed.

Most of the children need help to get dressed. As they grow, they become more independent and want to do it themselves. This can take time, but that is something we can provide. It does not matter if it takes a long time to put on a sock or trousers. Usually when given enough time the child will succeed, but we adults have the tendency to do it for them in order to speed up the process and, therefore we rob them of the chance to do it themselves. Later on, they might not want to dress themselves, although by then we expect them to, and they might need the help they did not want when they were younger.

> Pia is a girl who wants to dress herself, but does not always get it right. With a little help from the adult, she has the impression that she has managed by herself and is beaming with satisfaction when all the clothes are on and she can join the other children.

The children also get a piece of fruit and something to drink at this time, before they go out to the others. The time outside depends on how long the child has been sleeping, but everybody gets some time outside before they are either picked up or return inside for the afternoon meal. Weather permitting, they are allowed outside again after the meal and do not return inside until the end of the day.

> Pia loves being outside and the first thing she does is to look for her sister. Normally there is mutual joy when they see each other unless big sister Linda is busy with something special. Pia thrives outside in the sand pit, which is the most popular place. An adult is always present. She spends much time digging or filling the bucket with sand. In between, she walks around, but mostly with an adult or big sister. Pia is one of the children who stay until the very end of the day. If she has had a good sleep during the day, she is in a good humor throughout, but if she has had too little sleep, we notice that she is very weary in the afternoon. She is extremely happy when Mum or Dad comes to fetch her and her big sister. She waves goodbye to the educators smiling and happy, and sometimes she gives a hug to those close by.

Weekly and yearly rhythms in the kindergarten

Even though we don't have many different activities for each weekday, every day has its distinctive stamp. In the group for the youngest children the daily routine is made up of cooking and domestic chores and the menu is the distinguishing feature of each day. Cooking is our main activity and we have a bread day, a porridge day, a rice/pasta day, a soup day, and a baking day.

Monday is the walking tour day for the bigger children. The little ones don't participate, but still are very aware that today is excursion day. They watch through the window when the others set off with the adults. Sometimes we hear singing as they pass the window and many of the small children run to the window to have a look. The walking tour day also influences the atmosphere in the building. It is quieter with fewer children in the house. It is also noticeable when we go outside to play. We are on our own.

On the outing day, the little ones have Bread Day. On the menu we have bread and butter and delicious herbal tea.

On Tuesdays we have rice or pasta. Wednesdays is porridge day and also bread baking for the breakfasts. Each day is characterised by cooking that brings warmth and aroma to the room. There are always some children joining the adults at the pots, hence the need for lots of chairs around the place of activity. The adults work peacefully at the table or stove, while the children smell the food cooking and may even get to have a taste.

Thursday is our soup day. We prepare this in conjunction with the older groups. Vegetables are peeled and cut into small pieces with the little ones, while the soup is cooked outside on a fire in an iron pot. The bigger children are outside all the time, helping. As the little children get bigger, they are allowed to be outside while the cooking takes place.

Friday is baking day in all sections of the kindergarten. Every child who wants to can knead, taste, and smell the dough that finally becomes the best bread rolls. With butter they taste scrumptious.

The daily routines are more or less kept throughout the year, but when Christmas is approaching and the routine has been established, we have an "open day" on Fridays. Then all the children are allowed to visit each other across the sections. Most of the time it's the bigger children who come to visit the smaller ones. Only in spring we do see some of the little ones who are going on three venturing across. We take this as a sign that they might be mature enough to be moved up to the kindergarten itself.

The yearly routine is related to what is happening in nature and the cycle of festivals we celebrate. For festivals with the little ones, it's enough to make small changes, such as a flower on the table, a special tablecloth, or a new candle. We may dress up for a party. Perhaps we might have apple juice instead of tea or frozen strawberries in the drinking water, or a soft bun instead of bread. It doesn't take much. We simply mark the occasion by having something we don't normally have and something that is connected to the season. The adults' ceremonious and festive mood is enough for the children. We prefer to wait, and not force experiences on the children that will happen when they are mature enough to move to an older section. The atmosphere is felt by the little children, even though they don't participate. In some of the festivals it is possible for the youngest to be included in age-appropriate ways. For instance, the Thanksgiving meal in autumn is shared by all. At other times we just peep into the big section to see what's going on, and that in itself is rather exciting! ♡

Chapter Six

The Child's Play

The Child's Play

What is play? We often talk about "free play", but what do we actually mean by that? Many people have written about play and what it means, for not only the child, but also for the adult. Schiller writes: "man only plays when in the full meaning of the word he is a man, and he is only completely a man when he plays."[17]

He describes two forces we all possess, the force that forms and restricts and the force that gives us ideas and lets us flow into Fantasy. Play, or the *play force* as he calls it, combines the two and gives the balance that we need to function as human beings in the world.

Play is a foundation for life that is laid in childhood. A child who is active in play is usually healthy and well. A child who does not play is cause for concern. Play is the way the child expresses himself, discovers the world, and gets to know himself. There are many forms of play: playing with toys, acting, board games, computer games, and so on. Almost anything can be characterized as play. When we use the phrase "free play," it stands for an activity created by the child without any help from adults, as with the pre-formed rules of a game. Free play is "stand-alone" play where the *child* is in control. We notice quickly whether a child is genuinely playing or just passing time. A playing child seldom gets tired.

Waldorf education puts a high priority on free play, whether the children are playing inside or outside. Free play is the child's most important developmental tool, whether to discover new skills, work with experiences, or express happiness and sorrow. Free play encourages

---

17 Friedrich Schiller, *Letters Upon the Aesthetic Education of Man,* Letter 15.

children to develop as humans, physically, mentally, socially, emotionally, and spiritually, and therefore they need lots of time to play.

Healthy children play spontaneously, changing from one thing to another whenever needed. Play is made up of many things, including humor and seriousness. Play begins in the child's inner mind and each child's individuality shines through in the way she plays.

Infants and toddlers have several ways of playing. Play involving the body is connected to the sense of movement and sense of balance. Copying is linked to whatever the child sees, experiences, and imitates immediately. Social play comes into being with interaction with other children or with adults. Construction play is when the child builds with blocks or creates forms in the sand. All types of play give the child the possibility of exploring and practicing and managing skills.

The child psychologist William Stern wrote: "Every tendency to play is the dawn of the instinct for seriousness." He described the significance of the child's play and its importance for later development. Characteristics such as patience, exploration, creative zest, and social skills are practiced.[18]

Play is equally as meaningful to the child as work is to the adult. Through play, important learning processes take place. The result is not as important as the process itself. Sometimes we can see a reflection in the way we work as adults of the way we were played as children.

Role models and physical surroundings give possibilities for imitation, even though not all children's play is an imitation of something they have actually seen. The urge to explore is also very important. The child does not have to have seen something before wanting to do it. A child will pick up a spoon and start hitting a pot. The more noise it makes the funnier it becomes and it will be repeated again and again with much enthusiasm, even though it has not been done by others first. Children under three need toys that give them the possibility to explore by themselves. The toys must be so simple that the children have the freedom to change them into whatever they want.

Steiner writes: "If the children have [a doll made from a] folded napkin before them, they have to fill in from their own imagination what is necessary to make it real and human. This work of the imagination shapes and builds the form of the brain. The brain unfolds as the muscles of the

---

18 William Stern, *Psychologie der Frühen Kindheit,* p. 274.

hand unfold when they do work they are suited for. By giving the child the so-called "pretty" doll, the brain has nothing more to do."[19]

The power of imagination affects the form of the brain's growth, which takes place during the early years, and we are aware that the brain needs stimulation to develop. Our job is to find the right toys to stimulate and trigger the child's own activity, which in turn will encourage healthy development.

Toys and equipment for play

Children need toys, but not necessarily the type of toys that are true miniature copies of objects used in the adult world. With these toys, so detailed and perfect, there is no need for children to use their imagination to complete or add to the object. What they *really* need are toys that are so simple that they can be changed into whatever is needed in the moment.

Toys that stimulate movement, balance, and touch are very important for the little ones. This can include the furniture in the room as well as things like blocks and dolls. Toys should appeal to the senses and give children the opportunity to experience different types of fabric, quality, and color. The simplest toys and play equipment are often the ones that children are most attracted to. Small and large pieces of fabric, balls of knitted wool, simple cloth dolls, knotted dolls, doll's equipment, rocking horses, doll's perambulators and cradles, wagons to be dragged or pushed, small stools, benches that can be moved and used for building, small and large baskets, cups and vessels of wood or metal, ladles, knitted ropes, and rugs made of cotton and wool—all these things are playing tools for the little ones. We also often discover that they play with other things that we don't call "toys," such as a stick, a cork, or anything they find in the environment. Who hasn't watched a two-year-old sit and play with a length of wool for several minutes, then twiddle it around his finger, put it in his mouth to taste, and look at it again before finally putting it aside?

Adults need to make a conscious decision to select toys that are not just useful but are crucial for each child's development. All the time we ask ourselves, what exactly does this child need to continue his growth, and what can we do to strengthen the impulse to "linger" on a skill just learned? ᛞ

---

19 Rudolf Steiner, *The Education of the Child*, p. 20.

Chapter Seven

The Physical Environment

The Physical Environment

We attach great importance to the child's physical environment, both inside and outside. We aim for beauty in the environment, bearing in mind that for the little ones, the practical arrangements are as important as the aesthetic, in order to make everyday life function well. The physical environment must be organized to make sure that opportunities for movement and various age-appropriate challenges are in place. Children will make use of everything in their surroundings. Benches, tables, chairs and other movable furniture are ideal "toys" for children. All these things can be moved, examined, and explored without the risk of danger.

It is our responsibility as adults to choose what to have in the physical surroundings. We need to remove items that we feel children should not have, to make it a safe and secure place. In this way we do not constantly have to say, "No, you cannot do that." At the same time, we must not be so afraid that something bad will happen that we overprotect them. The child has to be allowed to explore the world even when there is the risk that she will fall off a chair. The physical environment should be a safe place with good boundaries to prevent injury, but at the same time allowing the children the freedom to face and overcome challenges.

The child needs to become familiar with the various qualities of materials and objects. In nature, the child perceives a world without boundaries. A garden will seem like a big world for a little child and she needs time to adjust and explore. Children are at one with their environs during the first years, and all their senses are open and receptive. Because of that, it is important that we set boundaries in the beginning, before we allow them to spread out into to new areas. Inside it is much easier to set limits. Ceiling and walls create a natural frame around the area to be investigated.

Human beings have been part of creating their environment, the world into which the child is born. This environment in turn has a deep effect on the child's development, because the child is completely open and unconditionally submits to and relies on his surroundings. The way we create the garden outside or the rooms inside depends on the "raw material" we have to work with, which part of the world we are in, what the children's needs are, and what resources are available.

The indoor environment

To begin with, we feel that it is important that the children and the parents are "seen" when they come into our kindergarten. The children must feel that they are welcome and that we are happy to see them: "We love being here." Of course, the same applies to the parents: "This is the best place for my child to be." The educators who greet the children and the parents are the ones creating the impression that this is a good environment, regardless of specifically how the physical surroundings are set up.

When we create the indoor environment we should try to have in mind how colors, forms, and behavior affect all of us, not only the children. For the adults the shaping of the physical setting is of great help and support in their everyday work. There are as many different solutions to creating a happy indoor environment as there are kindergartens. None are alike, nor should they be, but we get inspiration and ideas from each other and from specialists, where needed. It is important for us to know how the external world affects us and with this knowledge to see what is possible in any particular kindergarten.

The surroundings inside are of a very different quality from the surroundings outside. We know how being inside and outside affects us in different ways. What happens when we finally get outside after a very long day inside? We breathe out and expand in unrestrained relaxation and relief. On the other hand, if we have to gather for a specific purpose, the most natural thing is for us to get under a roof. We need somewhere that is a bit more restricted, a room where we do not "spill over."

We wish for the child to feel safe and warm in the room, and by choosing simple forms and tranquil colors, we establish just that.

Form and color

Form and color have a profound influence on the child. Their senses are far more open and exposed than in adults, and we need to take that into account when we choose colors in a room. We also want the child to remain in a dreamlike world during the first years and this influences our decisions. Calming, soft, and encircling forms make us dream, while busy, straight, and sharp forms wake us up.

I remember, from my own childhood, a night I spent at my aunt's. The wallpaper was very busy, with strong colors and different patterns and the whole wall was covered. I saw the shapes, but they became trolls and wild animals and I believed they were coming out of the wall. I closed my eyes, but could still see them and I remember being afraid.

It is, of course, different for each individual. We experience forms and colors differently and we do not know exactly how individual children will react. That is why it is so important to use colors and forms that are simple and neutral. A few calm colors are good for the sensitive souls as well as for the more robust. For the sensitive ones this is a necessity and the stronger ones can also need it. It becomes a contrast and counterbalance to our busy society. Everywhere the senses are being bombarded and strong colors and forms surround us in shops or on the street. Our eyes seldom get the chance to rest peacefully.

Large windows giving light are very important to those of us who live in a part of the world with long winters. In Africa, on the other hand, where the sun shines nearly all year round, it becomes very stressful when the sun shines all day, every day, day after day. People there try to protect themselves from the strong light and heat. During both the cold winter days in the North and the hot summer days in Africa, we have found that using pink or peach-colored curtains in the classroom is very effective. They soften the light and create a cosy atmosphere, whether it is cold or hot outside.

Rudolf Steiner talks about colors and their impact on the child:

Excitable children should be surrounded by and dressed in red or reddish-yellow colors, while lethargic children should be surrounded by blue or bluish-green shades of color. The important thing is the complementary color that is created within the child. In the case of red it is green, and in the case of blue, orange-yellow. This can be seen very easily by looking for awhile at a red or blue surface and then quickly looking at a white surface. The physical organs of the child create the opposite of complementary color, and this is what causes the corresponding organic structures that the child needs. If excitable children have a red color around them, they will inwardly create the opposite, the green; and this activity of creating green has a calming effect. The organs assume an inclination towards calmness.[20]

---

[20] Rudolf Steiner, *The Education of the Child*, p. 21.

This could be a guideline for us when we decide which colors we want to have to surround the child.

Rudolf Steiner has also given advice and suggestions as to which colors are especially suitable for different ages, especially in connection with schooling. Up to school age, he recommends a peach color. Ceilings and walls in a delicate color help bring harmony to the room. Patterned wallpaper can be disturbing. We need to rest our eyes on a surface that only has *one* color. We notice that the eye wanders about when there are different patterns and colors.

The question has been raised as to whether we should use black as a color in the kindergarten, and there are several opinions on that. Many associate the color black with the night, a hole, a nothing, or death. Color is experienced as a soul quality. In puberty a child can have a "black" period that may be expressed in various ways. In small children, we also see times where they want to draw and paint with the color black. What does the child want to express? Is it then correct to give the child a black crayon? The answer is to be found within you and the child concerned.

I experienced another way to look at the color black after having watched black children in South Africa draw themselves and others. Their despair was immense when they did not have a proper black to draw the hair. When we mix all the colors it does not turn black, but dirty, while the black color of a little girl's hair in South Africa is the most wonderful thing you can imagine. It would be difficult to find anything more colorful than the African culture and black is very much a part of everyday life.

Colors give us many different mood experiences, which are needed to have an abundance of stimuli and impressions. We feel that the use of color is a very important part of our teaching and that it gives us the opportunity to choose what we feel is right for "our" children.

The coatroom

On arrival at the kindergarten, the entrance hall or coatroom is the very first place anyone sees. That first impression sets the tone for the day. It is lovely if a little chest of drawers or a little table with a flower or a little picture catches the eye as you walk in, welcoming children and parents.

Here we must hang up our jackets and outerwear before going into the communal room. The coatroom is often the smallest room in the house, but it should really be one of the biggest so that there is space for many at the same time. This is the meeting place in the kindergarten. Everyone gathers here: children, parents, educators. The children are dressed here, and the need for space is strongly felt when there are so many children to be dressed at the same time. It can quickly turn into chaos unless we have a system. We need to know where everything belongs and to see that everything is put into its own place.

The coatroom needs to be clearly laid out so that the children can find their places easily. Each child has his own spot, usually marked with a picture next to his name. This simple picture may be a flower, an animal, or any other symbol that the child will easily recognize. Each child needs space for outerwear, slippers, and a basket with extra clothes. In addition, we need a place for rainwear and boots. A large carpet is useful to sit on when children start dressing themselves. Large chairs for adults to sit on are not only helpful, but also relieve weary backs that have to last many years. A notice board with information for parents hangs on the wall in the coatroom, because most parents pop in there when bringing and picking up the children.

The main room/kitchen

The main kindergarten room may be called the *kitchen*, since it is the heart of the kindergarten as the kitchen is the heart of the home. Here the most important things take place. A large kitchen area is essential and is placed where the educator can survey the whole room and observe what happens in every corner while preparing the food. For the children it is important that the room is well arranged, so as to be able both to easily locate the adults and to find their way around.

Food preparation tasks, such as preparing bread dough or peeling vegetables and fruit, take place around a large kitchen table. At the stove, an adult is stirring a pot and wonderful aromas, warmth, and sounds surround the children. There are tall chairs nearby so that the children can climb up and observe. We have to be aware of the danger of a hot stove, but having one adult who is watching all the time makes it like cooking at home. A small toy stove standing next to the big one inspires play. Our experience is that just as much food is prepared on the little stove as on the large one!

Chairs, tables and benches are used for climbing, pushing, pulling and building. In this room, it is useful to have several nooks and crannies as well. Children need places where they can hide; a cloth draped over the kitchen table will give rise to much fun and games. A large carpet on the floor where they can sit, lie down, roll around, turn somersaults, and crawl is ideal for encouraging play and movement.

Even though it is good to move things around, some things must stay fixed and constant and be there in the same place when the new day starts. Furniture and fixtures must be of good quality and secure. The room should not be overflowing with toys and equipment. Room is needed for movement, which is the main occupation at this age. We give the children the option of playing by themselves, next to each other or, as time goes by, together as a team.

The changing room

The changing room is a happy place to enter. This is the place where the child has one-on-one contact with the adult. The room does not have to be large, but it must have an intimate atmosphere and a pleasantly warm air temperature. We must remember that while we are fully clothed, the child will be undressed.

Everything needs to be practical and within reach. The changing table should be at the correct height for the adult. A stool in front allows the child to climb up onto it. Shelves for diapers and clothing and a large sink within easy reach are very important necessities. Having these means that we do not have far to move while changing and cleaning the child. This phase of the child's development passes quicker than we think and before we know it, the children are rolling around on the table or managing to stand up and there is a real danger that they may fall.

We need good lighting in the room and if possible there should be a window directly above the table so that the child can see what is happening outside. If we give ourselves the time to listen and look, we can see whether it is raining or windy, dark or light; we can watch the birds and the movement of the trees! This special time of caring for the child can also become an "informative" time. This is the time of day when adults have the most particular and close contact with each child. So if everything is in its place, this period can become very significant and enjoyable both for child and adult.

The sleeping room

This room is even more special and personal than the other rooms. The room should have a homely feeling even though more than one child will be sleeping there. Room for four beds is enough, along with one large chair where the adult can sit with a child on her lap if needed. In our toddler group we have two sleeping rooms with four cots each. Usually three or four children are sleeping outside, but if we wish we can add another cot to each room so that all the children are sleeping inside.

The window may have a deep pink curtain that gives the room a warm and subdued light, especially when the sun shines through. This room is never totally dark, even in winter. We make allowance for some of the children who need a little light in the room. Each child has his or her own bed with bedding brought from home. In this way, the children have something that looks and smells familiar, creating a safe haven. We recommend that in addition to the bedding, they also bring an article of clothing belonging to one of their parents. This has proved to be very successful for new children who are feeling a little insecure.

Each bed has a canopy made of light blue and rose-colored material, which separates it from the rest of the room and gives the child a sense of protection. On the wall behind the bed is a picture of an angel or something else with a peaceful and beautiful theme.

It can be useful to have a little table next to the chair for the adult, with a light and space for a musical instrument. This is sometimes needed to help the child sleep. Everything must be in place so that we do not have to leave the room for any reason.

The outdoor environment

The physical environment outside provides many sense impressions, along with opportunities for exploration and learning new skills. The child is starting upon an extensive road of discovery, using all the senses. The world outside is big and grows even bigger as the child moves around the kindergarten perimeter. An adult must be nearby all the time. It is sometimes important for a child to hold someone's hand while exploring. Of course, the outside area must be securely fenced so that after a while children can move around unassisted.

The sandpit is the center outside. Children of all ages gather here. The sandpit has, as a rule, a natural frame that designates a specific area, and they feel safe sitting there. Many forms of play take place in the sandpit and the sand has a quality that is useful whether dry or wet. The feeling of dry sand trickling through the fingers is different from that of the wet sand that can be made into sand castles or cakes.

With soil, which has a different consistency and color, something very different is experienced. Mixed with water, soil can be formed even better than sand can. Mud cakes turn into the most delicious cakes, chocolate and marzipan.

The smallest children often have enough to deal with in staying within the kindergarten perimeter. A sandpit and a limited area with a rugged terrain where they can strengthen and exercise their abilities are more than enough. Later, when they can control their own bodies and feel safe in the world of the kindergarten, they are ready to go out for longer trips.

The weather plays a major role in giving the children varied sense experiences. Rain trickling down in little brooks, discovering the water coming down the gutter pipe, standing with your mouth open to catch the raindrops—these are some of the adventures and experiences made in wet weather. Not all the water ends up in the mouth; much of it runs down the neck. After enjoying the feel of the water running into the mouth, the children suddenly realize that they are sopping wet, but *that* does not matter; there are (or should be) plenty of dry clothes and adults to help them change. The water experience can be prolonged in summertime when the children are wearing less clothing and the weather is warmer. Washing clothes outside is a wonderful activity, inviting happy participation by everyone. Most children love to play with water!

A secure and safe place for a bonfire is essential, a place to let the children experience fire, with flames crackling and the aroma emanating from different wood types. In addition to that, cooking outside contributes many good sense experiences and is an inspiration for children to play.

On one set day each week, we place a large iron pot on the fire to make soup, spreading a wonderful aroma across the whole kindergarten area. Sometimes we make pancakes, which offer a different sensation. Everyone is affected whether they stand around the fire or sit in the sandpit. The children learn that not only do we light a fire for relaxation and warmth, but also for cooking the food, which we will eat later. They do not need long explanations.

Cooking outside inspires the children's free play. Soups are made in the sandpit, in mounds of soil, under the gutter or under a bush. Leaves, stones, cones, and roots are used to make gourmet food. The warmth from the fire, the smoke rising, and the aroma of fire and warm soup all give diverse experiences for the senses. The little ones are allowed to have this experience when they are close to three years old, and we can see how they enjoy being outside with the older ones from the early morning onward.

In Norway we are fortunate to have four distinct seasons in the year, which give the child a profusion of sense experiences. As a rule, we can be outside most of the year, unless the temperature drops more than ten degrees below zero (Celsius). We just have to make sure that the children are dressed appropriately for the weather. In winter their clothes must be warm, but not so densely packed that they cannot move freely. Sometimes you can put on too many clothes. From experience we have learned that woollen clothes from inside to outside are the best, in addition to wind- and rainproof jackets. In other countries where it gets too hot, one has to consider when and how to protect the child against the sun and the heat. Even we, in summer, need clothes that are cool, and protection against the sun.

Apart from the seasons, a sense of *wonder* in regard to everything that happens and exists in nature is an important tool in dealing with children. Nature gives us many reasons to wonder, and the children are our teachers in this. The child has a natural gift to see what is beautiful and transform it through imagination—a drop of water on a leaf could be a pearl, or a pinecone look like a mouse. Adult consciousness meeting the child's awareness opens our own wonder about the little things around us. We marvel at a gray stone upon which the sun shines turning it into a beautiful stone of gold. There is an ocean of possibilities to wonder over in this world of ours. ♡

Chapter Eight

Models for Infant and Toddler Groups

There are various ways of setting up a kindergarten. It depends on who the kindergarten is being established to serve, where it is, and what the local requirements are. Once these things have been established the various possibilities can be worked on.

There are many alternatives like family kindergartens, sibling groups, and separate groups for the toddlers. Often kindergartens have more than one group catering for different stages and ages. I have chosen to highlight two possible concepts of which I have personal experience in Norway, and one possibility that I experienced in South Africa in one of the Townships in Cape Town.

Sibling group
A sibling group from birth to six years in Norway, with a maximum of 20 children, but preferably no more than 18. This group has one teacher and two assistants, all working full time.

The modern family today is complex and can be small or large. There are families with mother, father, and one, two or several children; single parents with one or more children, families where parents have children from a previous marriage, children living with grandparents or in foster care, and so on. Some have large families, others small. For many children growing up in a small family with no brothers or sisters, a sibling group could be a good solution.

In a sibling group the children have the opportunity to meet others of various ages and at different stages of development. This can be a reciprocal enrichment of play, as well as an opportunity for being together socially. The little ones will have more role models than just the adults. The bigger children receive inspiration for play through the spontaneous inventions of the smaller ones. Social skills are achieved by showing consideration for the younger children. Experiencing that the little ones get away with doing something that they are not allowed to do is very useful for the bigger children. At the same time they have the chance of showing care for and receiving love and affection from the smaller children. The youngest learn that there are things they cannot yet do, but they continue to strive until they succeed.

Sometimes it will happen that both groups have a need to be on their own. We often see irritation in the bigger ones if they have built something nice and a smaller one comes along and in ignorance breaks it down. When this happens it is not so easy to show care and consideration. The same applies to the smaller children; they also need to be on their own and play alone. The love shown by the older children is not always welcome.

If you have a group of twenty or more children together in one room, it sometimes becomes too much for the little ones. This is when it is an advantage to split the group, especially when the bigger children have activities such as painting, modeling, fairy tales or other activities for which the smaller ones are not yet ready. It is important to make time during the day when the two groups are separate and left in peace. The small children need protection, while the older children need challenges.

Toddler group within the kindergarten

A kindergarten with two groups, one from birth to three years and the other from three to six years, in Norway. In the younger group we have 10 children, in the older group we have 20. In both groups we have one teacher and two assistants. There is also a staff member whose role is primarily administrative. We are open from 7:30 until 4:15 and the teachers and assistants work from 7:30 until 3:00, or from 9:00 until 4:30.

This type of kindergarten opens up many possibilities and challenges for both children and adults. The co-operation between the sections can contribute and strengthen both the educational and the methodical in both sections, resulting in enrichment for all.

In their own area, the younger children will be able to play with each other without "help" from the older ones. In another area the older children can build their tall castles, without risking demolition by the younger ones.

With two sections in the house, each has the opportunity to be separate as a group, but also has the choice to be together. In our kindergarten, first thing in the morning, we are together. We chose to have a shared entrance, even though we have separate coatrooms. We have breakfast and the afternoon meal together, because not all children arrive and leave at the same time. These shared meals are taken in the section for the younger children. Afterwards the bigger children go to their own section. We deliberately chose to use the section for the little ones for the meals, because it is easier for the older children to move around from place to place. The younger ones feel safer being where they belong.

During outdoor playtime we also have the choice of being together or separate. The little ones have a playground directly in front of their section, but we often see them with the bigger children. Children seek each other out when they meet in outside play or in either of the shared meals. We have become aware that certain social skills are visible among the older children when they do not *have to* consider the little ones. We realize that the older children get more enjoyment out of helping the little ones or showing care for them when they are not together all the time.

One day a week we have an "open" house when the little ones receive visitors in their section. We open the doors and they can go where they please. Many of the bigger children love to visit the smaller ones. Here they have an opportunity to show care and to feel important when the help they offer is accepted. Broadly speaking the young ones stay in their section the whole year. Only when they get closer to being three years old do they start visiting the others on their own. This is the first sign that they are almost old enough to move up to the next section.

The advantage of this arrangement is that we can move the children between the sections if there is a need. We had a three-year-old boy who started in the older children's section. Everything went well in free play and activities. But when it came to storytelling time he had problems and battled with concentration. He did not really want to participate. Our solution, which took his developmental needs into account, was that he spent the storytelling time with the little ones for a few months, while the others in his group listened to stories. After a while, he was ready to take his place in the storytelling time once more, and was mature enough to really enjoy it.

Another little girl, also aged three, was still in the younger section. In some instances we could see she was ready for the move, but not in all. We solved that by letting her spend the free play time with the older children and the rest of the day with the small children. That was enough, and after a time, she was ready to move permanently.

This kind of decision is only possible if there is a good cooperation between the adults in the various sections. The adults must know the children of both sections well and be able to observe and understand what is happening in both. We are given a unique possibility of working together, using our creative talents. At the same time, the children meet more children and the prospect of diversity in play and friendships grows.

Infant and toddler group

An infant and toddler group in Cape Town. The number of children varies from 15 to 30, with most around 20, but ideally not more than 15. Often there is only one, maybe two teachers, and if they are lucky they have some volunteers to help out.

In many countries there are infant groups, children from birth to two years. In South Africa I have seen many of them, mainly in the townships. This group is usually in rooms separate from the kindergarten. There is no set number of children taken into the group; it varies from place to place. Depending on the need, sometimes they have fifteen to twenty, sometimes up to thirty children in one group. It is not ideal to have such big groups, but it is the reality in some places and many teachers have to deal with it.

I find that the children from one to three should be protected as much as possible from big groups, but see the value of bringing them together with the other group now and then. I believe the small child cannot cope with big groups over a longer period; they are in a period of development that they need space, tranquillity, and enough time to discover and explore without too many distractions.

The most important thing that anyone can give in groups this big, especially when facilities are not optimal, is the value of relationship and of meeting each child lovingly as often as possible. Many women are working hard with love and care to create a good start for children, not only in the townships, but around the world. ♡

Chapter Nine

Working with Parents and Other Caregivers

Working with Parents and Other Caregivers

Good relationships with parents, foster parents, and other caregivers are essential in the kindergarten. Reciprocal trust and confidence need to be in place. The children spend a great deal of the day in the kindergarten and co-operation with the home is of immense importance. There are several ways of meeting, either informally or by set appointments. The most essential is to create mutual confidence and awareness about what happens at home and in the kindergarten. Together it is possible to work out what is best for the child during his various developmental phases.

Teamwork between home and kindergarten

Teamwork starts the day the parents decide that their children are going to the kindergarten. It is vital that we have a mutual contract agreeing to exchange the experiences and knowledge that we have about their child and child development in general. The parents impart their insight and knowledge of the child at home, and the educator shares her experience and perceptions of the child while attending the Waldorf kindergarten. The child senses this fellowship. This can be very satisfying for the child. Both parties wish for the child to be happy and feel safe in the kindergarten. If the relationship is successful, everybody will be assured that the right choice has been made. On the other hand, should the parents feel uncertain, it will often be reflected in the child's pattern of behavior.

The kindergarten's responsibility is to receive the child and the parents in a way that inspires confidence. Communication is a very important foundation for the security we want to generate between parents and staff. When the educator explains the details of the daily activities in the kindergarten it will give the parents an assurance that all is well. In addition, when the educator explains the child's development according to the Waldorf philosophy it helps and supports the parents.

Children need parents who will give them scope to develop their own characteristics and help them accept their limitations. As parents and educators, we need to see the child's individual endeavors to explore and get to know the world. When a child arrives in the kindergarten for the first time, we are able to perceive something of the child's character at that first meeting, although we don't yet know her. The manner in which she separates from the parent gives us some indication, but not the whole picture.

Some children need a "breaking-in" period whereby one parent stays behind for a while before having to leave. Parents need this time for themselves and the child. Sometimes it becomes a power struggle between the parent(s) and the child and then it is helpful for us to intervene. There are no hard and fast rules on how to handle this, but by having a good relationship and trust between staff and parents, this problem can be solved in a sensitive way.

One way to help is to make a short call to the parents to let them know that the child has stopped crying. That can do wonders for the mother or father who had to leave while the child was still crying. Often the crying stops as soon as the parents are gone, but after they are out of earshot. Another way is to suggest that the parent stand outside, out of sight, and listen for the crying to stop. This makes it easier for the parents to leave the kindergarten.

Parents have chosen this particular kindergarten because it is the best for their children. It is an immense vote of confidence that the kindergarten staff takes very seriously. It is important that we remember our respective roles and that we as teachers neither can nor want to replace the parents, but we do want to be the best possible alternative for the child at this stage of their lives. The parents are always the ones who are closest and most important to the child.

Everyday conversations

Daily dialogue between teachers and parents helps to ensure the quality of the day for the child. Parents need to know what's happened during the day, and at the same time it is important for the staff to get a glimpse of what's happening at home. Chats face-to-face, on the telephone, or during previously arranged meetings give everyone involved an idea of how things are going.

Conversation can take various forms. A prepared meeting is different from the spontaneous talk that happens on the spur of moment while picking up or dropping off the children. We need both types of communication. There are two sides to a conversation, what we want to say and what the other side wants to communicate. The way in which we conduct the dialogue affects the outcome of the talk. We need to be aware of how important this is, so that we conduct the conversation in a caring way and make the cooperation with parents the best it can be.

An everyday chat is the form most used, and it is important to give parents the assurance that their child is safe and content. Often the child is present during these chats and we speak "over the head of the child." We must be careful to know what we can say while the child is present and what has to wait for later. Concerns that need deeper discussion and more time should be reserved for another time, but short messages or little anecdotes of daily happenings can illustrate that the child has had a good day. This is something parents need to hear, especially when the child has not yet learned how to communicate. At the same time the child will pick up on the contact between parents and staff and that will strengthen his sense of safety and belonging.

These daily chats also show the parents that we observe their children and are, therefore, able to pass on anything of importance that happens during the day. It is just as important that the staff be told if anything has happened at home. How did the child sleep? Did he eat breakfast? How was the morning at home before coming to the kindergarten? This can be communicated briefly without exposing the child. Short messages can be passed while the child is still sitting on mother's lap or just nearby, giving the child a sense of safety. The child will pick up the mood of the interchange very easily and notice the interest between the adults.

In addition we can use a little book for each child where we write down happenings of the day. That book stays on the shelf belonging to the child in the wardrobe. Parents can read it every day and if they so wish, can also use it to leave messages for the kindergarten. Sometimes it is not always convenient or appropriate to have a talk while picking up the child and then this is a good alternative.

Parent/teacher meetings

In most kindergartens parent/teacher meetings are held two or more times during the year. These are arranged so that we can get to know each other and ask questions about the welfare and development of the children. A meeting can take the form of questions regarding the situation at home or in the kindergarten. Or it may be a discussion concerning education or the practical work in the kindergarten. Sometimes it may concern the child's general happiness or well-being.

It is best that we get to know each other before the child starts in kindergarten. It gives the parents a chance to share information, such as details of the birth, the first few months, and the first year. All these things contribute to the picture of the child's disposition and are of great value in understanding and encountering exactly this child. This is usually done in separate private interviews with all the parents.

The educators describe what is important from the kindergarten's point of view, and why and how we do what we do. Home and kindergarten often seem like two different worlds to the child and our aim is to build a bridge between the two. If we succeed, it will be much easier for the child to shift between them. Our conversation often pertains to normal behavior and routines like sleep, food, and care or other everyday activities that happen both at home and in the kindergarten.

In all conversations with parents it is essential to create an empathetic space in which the parents do not feel threatened, but totally free to say what's on their minds. It is up to the kindergarten to create this ambience. A friendly, welcoming atmosphere, with tea or coffee, a lit candle, and comfortable chairs, is a helpful start to a fruitful conversation. Sharing experiences about the child is a good place to begin. As a rule we find common features. even though a child sometimes behaves differently at home and in the kindergarten.

The most important thing is to focus on the positive before tackling any problems. Normally, what is seen as problematic is actually just a phase the child is going through, as she battles to adapt to experiences and feelings that she cannot express in any other way. In order to understand what is happening, an account of the child at home and in the kindergarten is a start to find common traits. From that standpoint we can try to understand why things happen the way they do, and we can explore the question of what we can do to help. Could this be the so-called *defiant stage*? Personally, I prefer to call it the *independent* stage. That is not much of a consolation while it's happening, but remember, it doesn't last forever, and it is a very important step towards independence and freedom. Knowing that leads us to having more understanding than despondency. In fact, it is an occasion for rejoicing!

All kindergartens have organized gatherings with parents, which take a different form from that of the one-on-one meeting. At these meetings all the parents and staff come together and information that affects everybody is shared and discussed. Various subjects are brought up and discussed, one of them being the Waldorf curriculum. The educators are open to suggestions from the parents for the choice of subject, such as a concern about something important in society and its possible effect on our work in the kindergarten or at home.

We make space for questions and debates pertaining to the subject. The ideal is to create smaller groups to allow everyone to express an opinion and later come to a combined solution. If we succeed in creating interest so that the parents come with their questions and comments, we have achieved an important part of our work. Our job is to inspire the parents to take the initiative to learn more about a subject.

Parents and guardians are all interested in what their child does and what kind of day he has had in the kindergarten. It is very enjoyable when we include parents in what the child is doing, for example sharing songs and rhymes with movements. We can also share little stories or let them experience a taste of our celebrations. There are several ways to include the parents and give them an insight as to what their child's kindergarten life is like. We have to find ways to share and make it come alive for the parents. Whichever way we choose to conduct the meeting, we always make an effort with the setting. We light a candle, put a flower on the table, and serve a snack and beverage to help create a pleasant framework.

Meetings and conversations with parents not only support the rules of safety and security as laid down by kindergarten law, but they also help towards fulfilling the essential requirement that the children gain the best possible benefit from their kindergarten years. The parents are the main players when it comes to the upbringing of their child, but the kindergarten also plays a significant role.

There are other ways of getting together such as joint walks, voluntary communal work, open days, joint festivities, or an annual get-together where parents and staff meet without the children and get to know each other on a personal basis. How we chose to meet is not so important, but *that* we meet is essential. ♥

Chapter Ten

Working with Colleagues

Working with Colleagues

The staff members work closely together and depend on each other during a day that is usually filled with unexpected challenges. That's why the cooperation between them is as important as the connection with the family, even though it serves a different function. It is an advantage for the child if they complement each other and give children the opportunity to experience the diversity of the various adults in their environment. Closely knit teamwork based on mutual interest is a prerequisite for success. Working with young children is an intimate job and it demands the constant focused presence of the staff. Even though we might manage to leave our own personal problems at the door before we see the children, it helps if the other adults understand how we feel. In this way we can help each other without it affecting our work with the children. If the relationship between the adults is open, honest, and positive, and with plenty of humor, it will benefit the children.

In the beginning it is important and necessary for one person to have the primary contact with and responsibility for each child. That particular staff member takes responsibility for meeting the parents when possible, especially during the first few weeks. How do we choose which staff member this will be? It depends a bit on the "chemistry" between the child and the adults. We watch to see who the child gravitates toward and then we decide who is going to carry the main responsibility for that child. Our experience has shown that it is important for the child to establish contact and trust with another adult as well, so that if the main contact person is not there the child is greeted and held by the second adult. It must not become a burden for the child if his "security" person is not there; having to say goodbye to the parents is strain enough.

The staff strives to make contact with all the children in the group and after a while, children will simply turn to the nearest adult. Interest, care, and love are the basic foundation. If we add a bit of age-appropriate humor, we are even more equipped to be with the children. To be able to laugh together can be a relief if something goes wrong or not according to plan. This is also important for the adults; we too have days where things don't function the way we want. We must not take ourselves too seriously, but at the same time we do not forget the responsibility we have.

Cooperation between staff members is essential, as it is the pillar of support on which the kindergarten rests. We are all professionals in our field and work accordingly. That is expected by the parents and the children who have chosen to come to us. The children need not only our knowledge, but also to discover who we are as human beings—what we stand for, our attitudes, how we interact and how we solve daily problems together. This will give the child the foundation for her own social skills later in life. Together with parents and guardians we are a part of the child's upbringing. We become a supplement to the parents.

Daily teamwork

The staff's ability to work together is very important when preparing for the days and weeks of kindergarten life. Preparation of daily chores is a big job. We need to know who will do what and when. It quickly creates alarm in the room if any adult has to leave the room because she has forgotten something. Physical and mental presence is very essential. Allocation of daily tasks is done before the children arrive in the morning. Even though the main contact person has the primary responsibility for a particular child in the first weeks, the rest of us must be able to intervene when required.

In a way, we can be compared to the larger family of days gone by, when someone was always at home and the child grew up within the spirit of community, good and bad. In the kindergarten we have a small community, a fellowship where everyone has different chores, skills, and abilities. We have to prepare and coordinate what's going to happen during the day, in order to make it a safe and happy place to be. Not only *what* we do together with the child is important, but also our attitude and the way in which we carry out our actions and chores. In addition, we have to be aware of how we talk around the children. No matter how young, children pick up the nuances and mood of a conversation. Children have neither the need nor the ability to understand society's ills or any personal problems that might occupy the adults. If there is a need for that kind of talk, adults should make arrangements to have them afterwards when the children have gone home. Children have an uncanny knack of picking up our moods better than anyone.

Staff meetings

Since the daily chores in the kindergarten often consume the whole day, time for conversation and planning is often lacking, hence the need for regular staff meetings. If it is possible to have meetings after the children leave, everyone will be able to participate and that helps to strengthen the cohesion amongst the staff. The meeting should contain various aspects to enrich us in body, soul, and spirit. If the staff meetings are held in the afternoon, room for food and socializing should be made before the actual meeting starts. The meeting can contain study opportunities and touch on educational, artistic, and practical aspects. The study and educational topics further our education within the Waldorf philosophy. The artistic part of the meeting can be painting, whittling, modeling, eurythmy, or any other activity that gives us nourishment on the spiritual level which is so important in our daily work. We give our all to the children during the day and we need to replenish ourselves through creative activities. The practical part of the meeting gives us a retrospective look at the past week and "food" for planning the coming week.

We have chosen to start staff meetings with studies that last about one hour. Some staff members may have prepared and be able to read from a book or an article. When that happens, we may stop them and ask questions or make comments. Every fourth week we substitute our studies with an artistic activity. We try to make each meeting fruitful for all, not just another burden in addition to everything else we do.

Child observations are part of the meeting. We have chosen to concentrate on two children at a time, one from each of the two age groups. The staff present their observations, made over a certain period of time. Everyone is welcome to add or ask questions regarding that child. This is an excellent way of getting to know each individual child, including the children from other sections. Everybody has the responsibility and the opportunity to share pleasure, humor, or concerns regarding their group.

The final item on the agenda is to read a list of all the names of the children. One person reads out the names, giving us a couple of seconds to visualize that child. That way each child is "seen" by all of us each week and by everyone at the same moment.

Time for mutual encouragement, both during the day and at the meetings, creates a good working relationship that, in the end, benefits the children. Are we successful in seeing each other the way we see the children? We should complement each other, share responsibilities, and have fun. We should see the seriousness and significance in our work and experience the joy of fellowship with the children. If we succeed, we have reached a level which will give optimum benefits to the parents.

Conclusion

Working with very young children involves huge tasks and responsibilities. One is never sure whether one will succeed. At the same time, it is a privilege to be allowed to participate in the child's world.

Never at any stage of our lives will we find more trust, love, and wonder than in sharing those first years of a child's life. It is this knowledge that gives us the strength to continue when obstacles seem insurmountable. If we reciprocate with the same trust and love, we not only give the child the opportunity to educate himself, but encourage him to develop his own inborn skills and possibilities. Our task is to create the right conditions for these things to happen, and to give each child the freedom to choose what is right for his own particular development. Together with parents and guardians we will help the child to embark on his life's journey.

Knowledge of Rudolf Steiner's philosophy and teachings is of the greatest importance to us. This knowledge gives us the insight necessary to understand and recognize the character of the child. It helps us to accept and deal with age-related behavioral traits with sympathetic understanding.

Our Western world is a rich, informative, and informed society and because of this, it is very important that we maintain our compassion and our common sense. There are so many "experts" assuring us what our children need, so many offers and so much choice. If we succeed in sifting out the superfluous and highlighting the essential, we will have achieved much. In order to understand the child, we need to stand together and move forward in awareness. It is imperative that we observe and listen to the child and at the same time accept the value of the effect they have on us adults. We depend on each other and we learn from each other. We are forever changing and learning, especially through working with children. Children give us the opportunity to discover new sides in ourselves.

Of course knowledge is important when we meet the child, but the over-riding factor must be that we are, like the child, wondering and curious about that which exists in each individual. Wonder opens the heart to the surrounding world and to humankind's life and work. That is the way in which we create interest in each other and form the foundation for more humane interaction on a daily basis. Simply by virtue of being human individuals, irrespective of culture and society, we have much in common.

I would like to mention the women I have met in South Africa's townships, women who run kindergartens in squatter camps where conditions for bringing up children lack absolutely everything we of the Western world would take for granted for our children. I often wonder how, in spite of what you and I would consider materially inadequate childhoods, they have succeeded in becoming such wonderful people with so much enjoyment and love to share. In spite of their background they shine with such joy of life. Perhaps the reason lies just there: maybe they experienced love and warmth from the adults in their lives. It might not necessarily have been the parents, but perhaps some other person who made them feel important and appreciated at some point in their young lives.

Every look, every touch, and every positive action formed the basis for these women to stand out as responsible and independent people. It gives us hope that even one person can make a difference in the lives of so many little children.

In working with children under the age of three, we are given the unique opportunity of moving into a world we adults have long forgotten—a world of wonder and possibilities.

A quotation from Rudolf Steiner and a promise from Nelson Mandela and Graca Machel can stand as a model and aim for all of us working with children.

Each child in every age brings something new into the world from divine regions, and it is our task as educators to remove the bodily and soul obstacles, so that the child's spirit may enter with full freedom into life. These must become the three golden rules in the art of education; they must imbue the whole attitude of teachers and the whole impulse of their work. The golden rules that must be embraced by a teacher's whole being, not as theory, are these: first, reverent gratitude toward the world for the child we contemplate every day, for every child presents a problem given us by divine worlds; second, gratitude to the universe and love for what we have to do with a child; and third, respect for the child's freedom, which we must not endanger, since it is this freedom to which we must direct our teaching efforts, so that the child may one day stand at our side in freedom in the world.

—Rudolf Steiner, *The Spiritual Ground of Education*, p. 56-57

Our Promise to the World's Children

To our only children,

We write to you as a mother and a father, as grandparents and as great-grandparents, as politicians and as activists. You are the focus of our outrage, just as you are the focus of our hope.

You are our only children, our only link to the future. Each one of you is your own person, endowed with rights, worthy of respect and dignity. Each one of you deserves to have the best possible start in life, to complete a basic education of the highest quality, to be allowed to develop your full potential and be provided with the opportunities for meaningful participation in your communities. And until every one of you, no matter who you are, enjoys your rights, I, Nelson and I, Graca, will not rest. This is our promise.

—Nelson Mandela and Graca Machel, from the 2001 UNICEF Report *The State of the World's Children*

Bibliography

Aeppli, Willi. *The Care and Development of the Human Senses.* Forest Row, UK: Steiner Schools Fellowship, 1993.

Bainbridge, Nicki & Heath, Alan. *Baby Massage.* London: Dorling Kindersley, 2004.

Bjerke, Andre. *Fakkeltog.* Oslo: H. Ashehoug & Co., 1942.

Fyrand, Ole. *Berøring.* Oslo: Pantagruel, 2002.

Glöckler Michaela. *A Guide to Child Health.* Edinburgh: Floris, 2007.

Juul, Jesper. *Your Competent Child.* New York: Farrar, Straus & Giroux, 2001.

Keller, Helen. *The Story of My Life.* New York: Dover Publications Inc., 2001.

König, Karl. *The First Three Years of the Child: Walking, Speaking, Thinking.* Edinburgh: Floris, 2004.

—————. *A Living Physiology.* UK: Camphill Books, 1999.

Kulset, Nora and Frode Thorjussen. *Mamaliye: sanger fra et år i Sør-Afrika.* Trondheim, Norway: Musikkmarkedet, 2011.

Lievegood, B.C.J. *Phases of Childhood.* Edinburgh: Floris Books, 2005.

Lusseyran, Jacques. *Zwei Vorträge in Zürich.* Stuttgart: Verlag Freies Geistesleben, 1970.

—————. *Against the Pollution of the I.* Sandpoint, ID: Morning Light Press, 2006.

Mathiesen, Arve. *Barnet's Verden.* Steinerskolen Vidarforlaget, 1994.

Pikler, Emmi. *Peaceful Babies, Contented Mothers,* sixth edition. Budapest: Medicina, 1963.

—————. *Lass mir Zeit.* München: Pflaum, 2001.

Sanders, Barry. *A Is for Ox*. New York: Vintage, 1995.

Schiller, Friedrich. *Letters Upon The Aesthetic Education of Man*. In The Harvard Classics, Volume 32, *Literary and Philosophical Essays* (New York: P.F. Collier & Son, 1909–14). Ebook available at www.bartleby.org.

Soesman, Albert. *Our Twelve Senses*. UK: Hawthorn Press, 1999.

Steiner, Rudolf. *The Education of the Child and Early Lectures on Education*. Hudson: Anthroposophic Press, 1996.

—————. *Soul Economy and Waldorf Education*. Hudson: Anthroposophic Press, 1986.

—————. *The Foundations of Human Experience*. Hudson: Anthroposophic Press, 1996.

—————. *The Kingdom of Childhood*. Hudson: Anthroposophic Press, 1995.

—————. *The Work of the Angel in Our Astral Body*. London: Rudolf Steiner Press, 2006.

—————. "The Four Temperaments." In *Anthroposophy in Everyday Life*. Hudson: Anthroposophic Press, 1995.

—————. *The Spiritual Ground of Education*. Great Barrington, MA: Anthroposophic Press, 2004.

Stern, William. *Psychologie der frühen Kindheit*. Leipzig: Verlag von Quelle & Meyer, 1928.

Zimmermann, Heinz. *Speaking, Listening, Understanding: The Art of Creating Conscious Conversation*. Great Barrington, MA: Lindisfarne, 2004.

Appendix:
Two Lullabies from South Africa

from *Mamaliye: sanger fra et år i Sør-Afrika*, © 2011 by Nora Kulset and Frode Thorjussen. Used by permission.

Author's Note: *All over the world, mothers have always sung to their babies to comfort and soothe them. Before children are consciously aware of "meaning" in language, they respond to melody, rhythm, and sound. These two songs out of the wonderful singing tradition of South Africa will be enjoyed by children everywhere, as they have been by "my" children in Norway.*

About the Author

Eldbjørg Gjessing Paulsen was born in 1951 in Trondheim, Norway. She completed her Waldorf teacher training in Stuttgart, Germany. With three children of her own, she started Stjerneglimt Waldorfkindergarten in Arendal, Norway in 1984 and has been there ever since.

Eldbjørg works with Waldorf education nationally and internationally. She was the representative for Norway for twelve years in the international Waldorf early childhood association, IASWECE. She has taught various modules at the Seminar in Oslo, Norway, and has been a board member of the Norwegian Association for many years.

She spends time in Cape Town, South Africa every year helping with mentoring and teaching in the Townships, focusing mainly on the children under three years.

A Note on the Type

This book was set in Cronos, a typeface designed for Adobe by Robert Slimbach in 1996. It is an unusually warm and readable sans serif style that is derived from the classic forms of Italian Renaissance calligraphy.

The titles and ornaments are set in Alana, created by Pacfic Northwest designer Laura Worthington in 2011. Meticulously crafted after Worthington's own hand lettering, the font is named for her "darling little sister."

Made in the USA
Middletown, DE
13 January 2025

68761830R00071